Education for Life

Education for Life

J. DONALD WALTERS

ANANDA PUBLICATIONS
14618 Tyler Foote Road   Nevada City, CA 95959

Cover design by Bella Potapovskaya and Martin Benkler
Back cover photograph by John Novak

6 5 4 3 2 1
93 92 91 90 89 88 87 86

International Standard Book Number 0-916124-28-2
Printed in the United States of America

Contents

Introduction

For TWENTY YEARS I have served in various roles as teacher, guidance counselor, principal, college instructor, and consultant in public education. During that time I have participated in experimental projects for educational change, seen theories of education come and go, and read most of the current books on educational reform.

Among all the books I have read, *Education for Life* stands out as that rare pedagogical phenomenon: a book both refreshingly original and wholly workable.

Education for Life expands the current definition of schooling; it offers parents, educators, and concerned citizens everywhere techniques for transforming education into an integral process—one which harmonizes book learning with direct life experience.

This book recommends an already tested and proven system of education, one which emphasizes relevancy when teaching the "basics," and instructs children also in the art of living. As Walters states, this book has the further goal of helping people to "...see the whole of life, beyond the years that one spends in school, as education."

The unique perspective offered by the author will, I think,

give his readers a sense of discovery. Walters has taken seemingly difficult concepts, and offered simple definitions for them that are as convincing as they are unexpected. For example, he defines that seemingly vague word, maturity, as "an ability to relate to other people's realities, and not only to one's own." Immaturity he defines as "a little child throwing a tantrum on the floor because he can't get what he wants." Definitions like these stand out both for their simple clarity, and because they are exceptionally helpful. Parents and teachers will readily recognize them as being right on target!

Another thing I liked about this book: While profound, it is at the same time enjoyable to read!

Education for Life deserves to be read by dreamers and doers alike. Perhaps even dreamers, after reading it, will put it to use! For it offers direction for those people who feel that education should mean more than an acquisition of facts, more than intellectual exposure to a vast number of untested concepts, and more than a pragmatic preparation for employment. It is an exalted call for change, based on deep insight into the potentials of every human being. It tells us how to nurture creativity, wisdom, and intuition in each child, and how to tap his unexplored capabilities.

Jesse J. Casbon
Ed.D., The University of Alabama

Preface

THE TITLE OF THIS BOOK can be understood in two ways, both of them valid. Primarily, my purpose has been to recommend a system of education that will prepare children for life itself, and not only for employment or for intellectual activities. But I have also wanted to help the reader to see the whole of life, beyond the years that one spends in school, as education.

For if—as most people at least want to believe—life has purpose and meaning, then its goal must be to educate us ever more to the fullness of that meaning. And the true goal of the education we receive in school must be to help prepare us for that lifelong learning process.

1

Success Is Achieving What One REALLY Wants

HAVE YOU a growing son or daughter? If not, suppose you had one: What would you like him, or her, to become? A doctor? lawyer? scientist? business executive? or, if a girl who wants marriage instead of a career, the *wife* of one of these?

Most people want their children to have prosperity, a good job, the respect of their fellowmen. But most people's ambitions stop there. Their hopes are material and concrete.

Systems of education are directed largely by what parents want for their children. Because most parents nowadays want material success for their children, and success in the eyes of others, modern education is primarily directed toward helping students to achieve these ends.

Little attention, if any, is paid to making students successful as human beings.

How far might the present philosophy of education be carried?

I once read of a Mafia capo being kissed adoringly on the hand by a poor peasant woman—not, from what I could gather, for anything he had done for her, but merely because his thefts and murders had brought him great material power. And what mattered the sick conscience which was, one imagines, his constant companion? That was his personal problem. In the eyes of at least that peasant woman, and probably of many others, the man was a success.

We've all heard of, or met, wealthy people of dubious character who were more or less excused their "eccentricities" on account of their wealth. Such people are generally considered successful—the more so if their wealth was self-made.

But is it really success to attain wealth, if in the process one becomes universally disliked? I don't suppose anyone would seriously claim that it is.

Success is the attainment of what one *really* wants in life, and not getting what one merely fancies he wants. It is not earning a million dollars at the cost of everything that makes life worth living: happiness, love, peace of mind, true friends, inner contentment. Many a man has had to learn this lesson so late in life that no time remained for him to correct his mistakes.

Why then, from the beginning, was he urged down this wrong road?

For, of course, he *was* encouraged. Everything he ever learned—at school, in the home, from most of his peers—persuaded him that success lies in things tangible, not in such intangible things as happiness, or a good conscience.

Yet what do people really want from life? Money? Prestige? Power? Or the inner satisfaction they hope to achieve by these means? Put like that, it seems self-evident that what people really want is true happiness, and not the mere symbols of happiness.

Why, then, don't our schools teach those skills which will help students to find, not material success merely, but success as human beings?

12

Why don't they give them teachings that will mean more to them later in life than, for example, the story of how Henry V won the battle of Agincourt, or how the introduction of the longbow in that battle might inspire a search in present-day students for new techniques on the "battlefield" of modern business?

Why don't our schools teach human skills like how to get along well with others? how to get along well with *oneself?* how to live healthfully? how to concentrate? how to develop one's own latent powers or skills? how to be a good employee, or a good boss? how to find a suitable mate? how to establish harmony in the home? how to achieve balance in life?

I've been generous in suggesting that history teachers, in describing Agincourt, draw even business lessons from that battle for the deeper instruction of their students. Few indeed, if any, make more than the feeblest attempt at teaching practical, contemporary lessons from historic events.

Few mathematics teachers try to show their students how mathematical principles might help them in the exercise of ordinary logic.

Few English teachers try to instill in their students a respect for grammar as a gateway to clear thinking.

Few science teachers bother to show their students how they might apply what they learn in the classroom to creative problem-solving in daily life.

Facts! Give them facts! That is the cry. Cram as many facts as possible into their perspiring heads. The hope is that, if a student has any common sense left in him by the time he graduates, he'll know what to do with the great

13

mountain of data he has been forced to swallow during his undergraduate years.

This tendency to confuse knowledge with wisdom becomes a habit for the rest of most people's lives. Seldom has there been a more fact-gathering society than ours is today! And seldom has simple, down-to-earth wisdom been held in lower esteem. One's simplest utterances must be backed by a wealth of statistics, and supported by as many quotations as possible from the opinions of others, if they are to be considered even worth a hearing.

Because we equate education with a body of static facts, and because we see these facts as a preparation for maturity, we fail to recognize life itself for the opportunity—yes, the adventure that it is: the opportunity to develop to our full potential *as human beings.*

2

Does the End Ever Justify the Means?

YOU'VE HEARD that familiar rationalization of fanatics and "super"-activists everywhere, "The end justifies the means." Everyone knows it isn't true. A bad tree produces bad fruit. Evil means produce evil results.

And yet—suppose we restate the saying this way: "The end tests the validity of the means." This, surely, is a truth. For it is only by the actual outcome of a course of action that we can know whether or not the action itself was right and good.

Human deeds, even when well intentioned, are often wrong in execution. A man campaigning for peace may fight for his cause with such self-righteous anger that all he achieves is a disruption of the peace.

It is in the *outcome* of deeds that we see justified, or discredited, the deeds themselves: in the consequences of a theory that the theory is proved or disproved.

We see here the basic weakness of our modern educational system: It is more theoretical than practical. Far from trying to justify means by their end, it seems to see in ends of any kind a betrayal of the scholarly spirit. For ends imply commitment. And commitment suggests a lack of objectivity.

Formal education tends to remove itself from immediate and practical realities.

I am reminded of the case of a man of only grade school education, but of wide experience in mining engineering, who late in life decided to get a formal education. After much struggle he was able to persuade the authorities of a university to accept him on the strength of his years of practical mining experience. Some months later, to their disappointment, he quit.

"But why?" they demanded. "It meant so much to you to receive an education. And we worked so hard to make it possible for you."

"An education!" he snorted. "There isn't one of these professors who isn't teaching things that I myself discovered in the field. They are *my* students! What can I learn from them?"

Surely it is no accident that many of our greatest men and women—scientists, thinkers, teachers, molders of public understanding—either never finished formal schooling, or did badly in school. Einstein's teachers marked him for failure in life. Edison could only manage three months of formal schooling, after which his teacher sent him home as unteachable—as, in fact, "addled." Goethe found little in his formal schooling that he could assimilate; we are told that he failed to find a single study at his university that interested him.

What is the difference between great people and the pedagogues who explain the lives and discoveries of those great people to others? Simply this: that reality, not books about reality, is their teacher. Unlike the average pedagogue, they *are* committed to achieving specific ends, and are impatient of a system which seems almost to imply that the means alone justify the means; that method is more important than results; and that no conclusion can ever be final and had better always be labeled a theory.

However full a student's head is crammed with book learning, his understanding of things, and of life in general, after twelve or sixteen years of education, is largely theoretical.

Were we, on the other hand, with great scientists to define education primarily in terms of what *life* has to teach us, we would soon find reality directing our theories, instead of theories molding our perception of reality. As it is, students are seduced into championing the most hare-brained, even dangerous, beliefs, all because their teachers are too "objective" to mind if a theory offends against rudimentary common sense, so long as it is presented attractively wrapped in intellectual tinsel.

Take, for example, the teachings of Jean Paul Sartre on the meaninglessness of life. Because his theories are intelligently worked out and well written, they are offered at the universities as standard intellectual fare.

A recent survey of professors found that the vast majority of them preferred wordy, intellectually intricate and difficult-to-understand articles on subjects in their own fields to articles that made all the same points, but in a style that was simple and easy to read.

The people who conducted the survey then took clearly written articles, and restated them in abstruse-sounding, pseudo-intellectual terms. These re-written articles, when compared to their originals, the professors almost unanimously voted better researched, better thought out, and more insightful.

It is astonishing the extent to which the theories learned at school, and even more so at college, can impose in later years on one's perceptions of reality. This isn't meant to sound drastic. Indeed, I would counsel most intelligent young men and women to complete their formal education, deficient as it is. It is to the *deficiencies* of our system of education that this book is addressed. No attempt is implied to damn the entire system.

But what of the psychologist who insists, everybody's practical experience (including his own) to the contrary, that the mind of a newborn baby is a blank slate waiting to be written on by his environment before he can develop his own personality?

What of a Freud, who tried to explain all human motivation in terms of the sex drive? (I can imagine physicists trying to fit Freud's theory to their own urge to discover a quantum theory!)

Educated people, far more than those who have been raised in the "hard school of life"—which is to say, of common sense—are notoriously prone to mistake theory for reality.

If education is to address life more realistically, and actually to prepare children to meet life's exigencies and opportunities, then it must be seen in the context of a constant learning from life, and not of a fixed body of knowledge that is passed on from one generation (already, in its own eyes, fully educated) to the next. It must be seen as springing from life and reality themselves, and not from carefully worked out theories about life and reality.

It must, in other words, be experiential, and not only theoretical.

It must protect students from the trap into which so many intellectuals fall: the belief, namely, that a theory's fascination is its justification. In this sense the student should be taught always to look to the outcome of a course of action—to the actual end of every means.

In this simple attitude of mind may be found the seed from which can be evolved what is here proposed: a new, and revolutionary, system named, *Education for Life*.

3

Harmony
with Life

GALILEO ONE DAY OBSERVED the swaying of the great candelabra in the cathedral of Pisa. His reflections thereon led to his discovery of the law of pendular motion.

Newton one day observed an apple fall. According to Voltaire, this observation led to his discovery of the law of gravity.

All science is discovery. And the glory of the scientific method is that, shunning a priori assumptions, it insists on observing and learning from things *as they are.* The true scientist tries never to impose his human expectations on objective reality.

That he has human expectations, and that these expectations sometimes impose themselves on his findings even without his intending them to do so, goes without saying. Even Einstein, disagreeing with the great physicist, Sir Arthur Stanley Eddington, on some abstruse matter of science, concluded that, after all, it was really only a matter of taste.

Scientists too, after all, are human. It needn't dismay us too much to find them occasionally, as human beings, out there in the pit of competition, even, slinging mud with the best.

What *is* dismaying is the widespread assumption that, if one can only train oneself to become completely scientific in his outlook, he may so far rise above his human feelings as to remain always coldly objective—a sort of superman, because always in tune with *what is*. Or, to put it in other words, a sort of shock-proof watch, because protected in his mental ticking from any extraneous, outside influence.

A great deal of modern education is directed toward perfecting students in the scientific attitude: toward teaching them to transcend all human expectations and desires and to view reality, and life itself, with pure intellectual objectivity. Inevitably, the suggestion passes from transcendence of human expectations to transcendence of humanity itself.

It is no accident that so many fictional glimpses into the future of mankind reveal a world stripped of such "extraneous" concepts as beauty, kindness, happiness, and—one suspects—the first of all to go: humor. Most science fiction, as a prime example of this genre of literature, is depressingly sterile, mechanical, and lifeless. Earth, as it is shown to us hundreds of years in the future, is a place without trees, without grass and streams and singing birds—a place where science has finally collared Nature and made her sit down and behave herself; a place, in other words, of concrete, steel, and plastic, of efficient laboratories and smoothly functioning machines.

A famous psychology professor used to tell his classes, "If any of you thinks he has a soul, please park it outside the door before you enter this classroom." Cute! And, of course, it got him the titters for which he was fishing. What he was saying was, Let's approach our subject with intellectual objectivity—scientifically, and without pretensions.

But what he was also saying was, To be scientific, we

psychologists must view human nature as the physicist views matter: as a thing, merely, a collection of molecules that is conscious only because matter, in the long, meandering process of evolution, happened to produce a brain.

In this view of human nature, it is of course absurd to suppose a soul.

But in this case, it is equally absurd to suppose ideals, to encourage fantasy, to reach *up* toward anything at all— only *outward,* toward the "gut-level" satisfaction of instinctual, animal desires.

S. Radhakrishnan once, when he was vice president of India, said to me, "A nation is known by the men and women it looks upon as great." In the light of this wise statement, does it not seem sometimes as if the model we were being offered of the Ideal Man were something akin to a robot?

In how many modern novels do we find the hero described as smoothly efficient, unemotional, finely tooled physically and mentally—like a machine. For these qualities we are expected—not to like him, perhaps; that would be asking too much: but at any rate, to admire and respect him.

Intellectuality that is not balanced with feeling tends to develop a Hamlet complex. That is to say, it has a tendency to paralyze action. Professors, with the excuse of objectivity, but in fact more because of an excessive dependence on the intellect as a tool of understanding, incline toward uncommitment. In this respect they differ from the truly great scientists of our era.

Einstein said that the essence of scientific inquiry is a sense of mystical wonder. Every great scientist, like every great human being, is a dreamer, a person of vision, and a person *committed* to his vision. One thinks, here, of Edison, testing sixteen hundred filaments before finding one that would work in an incandescent lamp. Imagine such total commitment to what must have seemed, at least to everyone else, an improbable end!

And how different the great scientist, in this respect, from the average professor pretending to represent him in the classroom! More or less forgotten by the time the scientist's findings reach the textbooks is his own probable disinterest in a great deal of what the classroom represents.

It seems likely that the pedagogues, with their fondness for intellectual uncommitment, are partly responsible for the frozen image so many people hold nowadays of the ideal human being. Our school system breeds a preoccupation with things, and with abstract ideas, but an indifference to human values.

Psychology itself, however, tells us that human nature cannot be suppressed. Ignore a person's emotional life, instead of trying to develop it along constructive lines, and it will merely find other, destructive outlets for its energies.

Look at television—that mirror of public attitude and opinion. One has only to turn on a television set to be confronted, probably within the first five minutes, with examples of almost embarrassing immaturity. Screams in anger, insults to others, striking out with fists and feet, a refusal to listen to the simplest common sense, even shooting at others—this type of behavior is presented as if it were more or less normal. Selfish indifference to the needs of others seems to be quite taken for granted.

In terms of scientific achievement, we may indeed have something in which to pride ourselves. But I wonder, after a lifetime that has taken me to many countries in different parts of the world, whether Western civilization hasn't started producing people of stunted development as human beings.

I am reminded of the question that was once posed Mahatma Gandhi: "What do you think of Western civilization?" Gandhi's reply, given with a smile, was, "I think it would be a good idea!"

Science has provided an important key: Don't impose your preconceived notions on nature; listen, rather, to what nature has to tell you, and harmonize yourself with that. Nothing in this dictum limits one to intellectual research alone.

Why not seek to harmonize oneself with nature on all levels? Why not try to learn from life itself the things it would teach us? Science has taught us to learn from nature. It is time now that we addressed ourselves to seeing what we can learn from human nature.

This is not rightly the task of our school system, any more than scientific discovery is its task. The purpose of schooling is to pass on to students what has been learned outside the classroom, in the great school of life. But much has been learned already through the millennia about human nature, and of the ways one can find personal fulfillment in life. The need, simply, is to include these findings among the subjects covered in the classroom.

The need, moreover, is to approach these findings with the same objectivity that has proved itself so essential in the investigations of science.

From life itself must be drawn the lessons that can help mankind to live life better.

4

How Progressive Is Progressive?

Much ENERGY HAS BEEN DEVOTED so far to discussing the needs of higher education. I am aware, however, that for most people the greatest concern is with the very young. It is my concern also. For it is during a child's formative years that he develops those attitudes and assumptions which will remain with him, to condition his understanding for the rest of his life.

It is, however, from the higher levels of education that teaching in grade school is developed—just as it is from the educated adult population that teaching in the universities is directed. Thus, it is important to approach the subject of education from above, not below.

Indeed, the important thing is first to convince *adults* everywhere of the need for a fresh approach to education; then to convince the teachers. After that, the children won't need to be convinced—not, at least, the younger ones. What they will need is to become involved.

Does this statement set a few teeth on edge? There are few areas in life more susceptible to dogmatism than child education. And there are few dogmas more persistent than that of childhood's "natural" wisdom. It is something akin to Rousseau's "noble savage," a mythical creature for which most of us feel a strong, but—let's face it—largely unrealistic, attraction.

Yes, of course, children often display an astonishing measure of natural wisdom. We've all learned from them. Natural, uneducated man, too, knows many things that become lost in civilization's shift toward the refinement of knowledge. There is truth indeed in the oft-voiced belief that the child can teach the adult. But this truth stops far short of the next point many adults like to make, namely, that children should determine what it is that they want to learn, and be taught primarily that.

"Progressive" education, as it was named decades ago, seems in many ways to have been a step backwards—from order to chaos.

I don't intend here to deal with the issue of discipline vs. permissiveness, though that is certainly a problem raised by permissive education. But what I want to emphasize is how important to the term *progressive* is the simple concept, *progression*.

For the point is, the learning process is expected to take one *from* somewhere *to* somewhere: from relative ignorance, that is to say, to relative understanding. One can't begin with the poetic assumption that it's the adult, really, who will do the learning.

I heard a poet once address a large audience with the words, "I don't know what I'm doing up here. You all should be up here, teaching me. And I should be sitting down there in your place."

"Come off it!" I thought, as I left the room. "If you really mean what you say, then why don't you just get down here with the rest of us?"

We all know, of course—if we aren't too lost in dogmatic rationalizations—that the child will have, sooner or later, to pick up such abstract subjects as arithmetic, a few fundamentals of physics, and a knowledge of how to read. He wasn't born with these. "Progressive" dogmatism has a field day, however, when it comes to moral, religious, and simple human values.

"We don't want to impose our values on the child!" comes the warning. "He knows what's right for him. Let him decide what he wants to believe."

Dogmatism increases in direct proportion to one's inability to prove a point. And in these less fact-oriented subjects, many feel, the coast for dogmatism is clear.

Meanwhile, because modern mankind's ethical development is failing to keep up with his scientific advancement, the human race stands in growing danger of bombing itself to heaven—or wherever.

Are our children really able to teach us the secrets we need to know for our racial survival? That little one who lispingly pleads with his parents, "Mommy, please, please love Daddy! Oh, Daddy, *please* give Mommy a kiss!" may indeed have chalked up one for international peace. But his victory is just as likely to be canceled out a few minutes later by a shout to his sister, "Give me back my toy!"

Imagining children to be already fully themselves on basic issues of behavior and belief, we let them grow up without guidance in these matters. Later, we wonder why it is that so many of them grow up emotionally immature, and with faith in nothing.

The very educative process, especially in the upper

27

grades of high school and in college, is so directed as to strip a child of whatever faith he might have had.

One of the dogmas of modern thought is that life is essentially meaningless—scientifically speaking, of course; but our children get the message. Evolution, they are told, is an accident born of a long series of haphazard "sports" of nature. Everything, according to science, is relative; moral values, therefore, are relative also. Evolution is not progressive, for it has nowhere to progress to; it might as easily have brought life to a kind of mammalian dinosaur, stupid but invincible, as to the present rulers of the earth, the human race.

As one psychologist put it, "Has mankind evolved more in producing a brain than the elephant, in producing a trunk?"

Be that as it may, if the best we can give our children is the conviction that there is no real purpose in anything—a dogma nowadays—we mustn't be too suprised if they retaliate in anger.

The present generation seems almost *born* to destroy—and to be destroyed.

A growing child requires faith almost as badly as he requires air to breathe. When you strip him of any faith, his disillusionment turns almost inevitably into a desire for vengeance against those who deprived him of faith.

Our teachers have talked long and patiently to the children about the merits of objectivity. But is it objectivity the children are learning? They've been taught to sneer at emotional subjectivity, as if by rationalizing emotion they might transcend its deluding influence. But how much has really been accomplished? We've got them to suppress their emotions, but now we find those emotions breaking out in countless irrational ways.

That delightful children's fantasy, *The Never-Ending Story,* makes an important point: when fantasy is suppressed, it resurfaces in the form of lies. Emotions suppressed, similarly, reduce one's ability to handle life realistically.

What then? Surely it is time we kept in their own place all those scientific abstractions, and paid attention to other rooms in our house of earthly experience. I don't mean to ignore those abstractions. Certainly, they have their place in this house also. But let them keep to it. Let us not allow them to take over the entire edifice.

Surely it is axiomatic that we want our children's upbringing to be progressive, in the sense of leading them *somewhere.* But where? Leaving all those abstractions aside, isn't the simple, obvious answer: from immaturity to maturity? Isn't that really what growing up is all about?

Very well, then: What is maturity?

Simply put—and truth needs to be simply put—it is *an ability to relate to other's realities, and not only to one's own.*

What is immaturity? It is a little child throwing a tantrum on the floor because he can't get what he wants. Growing up is learning that life won't just give you what you want: you have to learn how to play the game. This is called adapting to reality, and many immature people call it compromise, though it is no more compromise than Edison's was in accepting the fact that only one filament, out of hundreds, was capable of lighting an incandescent lamp.

29

Many people never mature very far beyond the level of the little child prone to throw a tantrum every time his desires are thwarted. Much might be done during the growing-up process to cure them of this infantilism. But instead, the very dogmas of our adult world tend to feed, not cure, the delusion.

Not long ago, during a recession in Detroit, many hundreds of workers had to be laid off. As many as possible were given psychiatric counseling to help them to adjust to their new reality. But because the unemployed were many, and the counselors relatively few, many of the former had to go without counseling.

Interestingly, those who received counseling had a much more difficult time adjusting than those who did not. Encouraged, one imagines, to dwell on their misfortune in an effort to get them to see it objectively and thus cope with it, they only focused energy on their problem, instead of getting on with the task of finding a solution.

Maturity is not a finishing line, reached at the end of a race. It is a continuous, one might even say eternal, process. For who may ever claim, "There now remains no reality to which I cannot relate"? Who, indeed, knows where the ultimate horizon lies? One sails toward it until he discovers that he has circumnavigated the globe.

Much of this book will be directed toward helping children to find their way *progressively* toward what might be called the goal, not only of childhood, but of human existence: true maturity.

5

Sartre vs. Jesus

"GNOTHI SEAUTON," proclaimed the inscription at the Delphic oracle: "Know thyself."

"The proper study of mankind is man," Alexander Pope wrote.

"This above all," said Shakespeare through the mouth of Polonius, "to thine own self be true."

How many times throughout history has mankind been counseled to turn within, if he would achieve wisdom. His very ability to relate successfully to others depends first of all on inner self-development. As Shakespeare put it, to conclude that last quote, "And it shall follow as the day the night, thou canst not then be false to any man."

It is this eternal truth—this *wisdom*—that has been swept aside in the modern rush toward scientific discovery.

And yet, even scientific discovery has not been granted to every scientist. We see that, in certain respects at least, the greatest scientists have also been great human beings—and not great merely because of an exceptional intelligence. (There have been far too many intelligent idiots in this world for intelligence, per se, to be considered a mark of greatness!) They were great in a fuller and deeper sense.

31

For one thing, they had—at least in their dedication—the ability to rise above petty self-preoccupation and embrace a broader vision. Lesser persons—including, of course, lesser scientists—have not shown such an ability; most likely, they have not even wanted to do so.

Motivation is one of the tests of greatness. Lesser persons are, almost by definition, motivated by the thought, "What will I get out of this?" The greater the nature, the more expanded it is, and the greater, therefore, its indifference to personal gain. There have been great scientists, certainly, with mighty egos and considerable personal ambition. But in their work, at least, they have been able, better than most of their colleagues, to lift themselves above such petty preoccupations.

Great scientists, again, have been clear enough in themselves to be able to focus all their energy and attention on the tasks at hand. Lesser men haven't this power of concentration; they lack, therefore, that extra quality of intuition which leads to great discoveries. For intuition is always the product of calm concentration.

Luther Burbank, the famous botanist, would be inwardly so mentally one-pointed during his experiments with plants that his eyes would actually remain half closed and half open. Other botanists couldn't even duplicate some of his experiments, let alone rival them.

Who knows whether insight even into the workings of the cosmos doesn't depend first on a measure of self-knowledge.

Pythagoras, the Greek sage, lived at a time when civilized man had neither the means nor the vision to think of the universe as anything but geocentric—that is, as having the earth for its center. Yet Pythagoras taught that the earth is round, and that the stars, sun, and planets, including this earth, revolve around a great central fire. His explanation of things is astonishingly similar to that of modern astronomy, which has discovered that all the visible stars belong to a single, vast galaxy, revolving slowly around what might be described as a fiery center—packed as it is, from our distant point of view, with billions of stars.

Whence that ancient sage's amazing insight? No theory so vast, surely, could spring from the perceptions of any but a vast nature.

In this Twentieth Century a great deal has been written, albeit somewhat superficially, on the importance of knowing oneself, and of being true to that knowledge. Nora, in Ibsen's play *The Doll House,* was one of the early examples. So also was Kate, in J. M. Barrie's *The Twelve Pound Look.* Both women chose to live self-reliantly rather than continue as slaves to their insensitive and patronizing husbands.

In more recent years, the body of this sort of literature has been growing, along with hundreds of classes and seminars on techniques of self-fulfillment.

It would be no great step, then, to bring this emphasis into the schools and onto the campuses. The process is, no doubt, already well under way.

The question to be asked is, How, really, may one know oneself?

Is it enough to follow the lead of Kate and Nora?—to stand up to society and to one's peers and cry, "From now on, I'm going to get mine"? More than this, surely, is called for.

One of the best exponents of the "get mine" philosophy was the existentialist, Jean Paul Sartre, who claimed we should assume that we *are* our basic desires. If, therefore, according to him, we can strip ourselves of all extraneous influences—of society, family, and associates—and be true to that intrinsic nature, we shall find the personal fulfillment we crave.

The writings of Sartre have been avidly studied, as though they were actually important to human development. And yet the simple fact is, he was a nihilist. He accepted no norms. He claimed that if it is a person's intrinsic nature to rob, cheat, and kill, then, regardless of what anybody else thinks of him, he should pursue that path.

Nor was the man joking. He wrote a book about an actual person, Jean Genet, a thief and male prostitute, and titled it, *Saint Genet.* Why *saint?* Because Genet had the glowing "integrity" to admit boldly all that he was, and to act accordingly.

No, Sartre was not joking. Nor is his influence on modern society a joke. One sees that influence at work in the behavior of countless young people today—people who loudly proclaim the meaninglessness of human life, and who behave with egocentric abandon.

One wonders: Why have such teachings been given so solemn a hearing in the classroom, while there exists a vast body of time-tested teachings on the subject of true self-fulfillment that remains virtually ignored?

Sartre's grotesque distortion of man's quest for fulfillment at least makes it very clear that an affirmation of the ego is not at all enough, and that this cannot possibly be what the ancient sages intended. For greatness has always been understood to mean an expanded nature, a broadened sympathy, which, far from setting oneself against others, includes their well-being in one's own.

Consider all the great teachers of mankind—Buddha, Krishna, Moses, Jesus Christ. Their teachings receive hardly a passing nod in the classroom. Why this lack? Is it merely because those great men are "old hat" now, in this era of enlightenment? Let us hope our professors are not being merely faddish in their rejection.

A more likely explanation for all the attention given to nihilists like Sartre, and the virtual absence of it to great teachers like Jesus, is that the nihilist issues no call to action; he laughs at commitment of any kind, and is much more interested in clever theories than in truth. In this respect he is not unlike many a professor. Jesus, on the other hand, and those other great teachers, began and ended their message with a call to action, to total commitment.

I have had occasionally in my life the responsibility for developing projects that involved the cooperation of others in the service of an ideal. And I have observed that there were always some people who, out of what I think must have been too intellectualized an idealism, seemed actually to resent practical solutions to problems. Action—commitment—these, to them, seemed too gross an invasion of the rarified atmosphere of theoretical perfection in which they aspired to live.

Such people, even should they follow a Jesus or a Buddha, would do so only because that great teacher is no longer around to tell them to keep their feet on the ground.

The common explanation, of course, for not including

spiritual teachings in the classroom is that formal education is concerned with imparting demonstrable realities, and not with dogmatizing students in unproven sectarian claims.

It is, I grant you, a bit much to hear people speak of *Christian* humility. Why the special publicity? Why not, simply, humility? Is humility in some subtle way less humble when practiced by a Buddhist?

But humility, as such, is by no means an untested teaching. It doesn't take much living to see that pride goes, as we've often been told, before a fall; and that humility, when rightly understood, attracts success.

There are countless wise teachings that have been handed down through the ages, and that are products of the deep and universal experience of the human race. Such wisdom has nothing to do with religious sectarianism.

If even scientists require at least a touch of greatness to be perceptive enough to make great discoveries, then it is not enough, surely, for us to study their discoveries alone. What our schools need to offer is also a study of what *made* them great—or, more to the point, of what constitutes true greatness.

6

Punishment and Reward

RELIGIOUSLY INCLINED PEOPLE have long lamented the influence of science on religion. *Thoughtful* religious people, however, are grateful for this influence. For although traditional dependence on belief as the criterion of religion has been knocked head over heels, science has also offered a better alternative to blind belief.

How useful, indeed, even to religion is blind belief? And how credible is a belief system that cannot be tested?

It was once a universally accepted belief that the earth was flat. Christopher Columbus disproved this belief. Now, of course, everyone—with the possible exception of members in good standing of the Flat Earth Society—knows the earth to be round.

Dogmatism has traditionally sought support by appealing to reason. Numerous religious tenets have been defended against opposing beliefs, and sometimes even against the commonest of sense, by weighty theological treatises. By thus resorting to logic, religion has tried to avoid the stigma of blind belief.

Science recently, however, has weakened reason also as an arbiter of truth. In so doing, it has undermined still further religion's traditional assumptions. For what science now claims is that reason is unreliable if it is not substantiated by experiment—which is to say, in the human field, by experience.

Take, for example, the Michelson-Morley experiment with the speed of light. One might think it a point too obvious for dispute that the speed of light depends on the relative speed of its point of origin—even as a ball, thrown forwards from a car traveling sixty miles per hour, will travel the speed of the throw *plus* those extra sixty miles per hour. Obvious, isn't it? And yet, the Michelson-Morley experiment proved that the speed of light is constant *regardless of* the speed of its point of origin.

Impossible! And yet, for all that, experimentally proved.

Repeatedly, science has demonstrated the inadequacy of both reason and "common" sense.

In matters of religion, of course, mankind has been accustomed for centuries to accept a body of beliefs that often defied common sense. It is this scientific attack on reason—theologically the last court of appeal—that has dealt conventional religion such a staggering blow.

Not surprisingly, the churches have fought back with every anathema they could muster. Yet there is a good reason why those thoughtful religious people referred to earlier feel so differently.

In all things, the only thing that really serves mankind in the end is the truth: the state of things *as they are*. Didn't Jesus himself say, "Ye shall know the truth, and the truth shall make you free"? It is a repeated error of the human race to be afraid of truth. What kind of "belief" is it, indeed, that refuses intelligent challenges?

Orthodox religion has been quite as much to blame as our educational system for the lack of moral teaching in the classrooms. Why all this clerical insistence on blind beliefs? Even if we grant that there are many Scriptural teachings that cannot be tested, there remain countless others that can and that jolly well should be. How else will they ever become meaningful to us?

Jesus said, "By their fruits ye shall know them." And St. John wrote, "Try the spirits whether they are of God." It is unimaginable that any true teacher would ever demand mindless obedience of his disciples. Jesus told the woman of Samaria, "We *know* what we worship." He didn't say, "We *believe* what we worship." If we are ever to attain to a similar level of knowledge, we must be willing to test our beliefs as he himself urged us to do.

Admittedly, we may lack the means to test such articles of transcendent faith as the belief in angels, or in a life after death. These are hardly pressing classroom issues, anyway. But there is still plenty of good stuff in the Bible, and in other great Scriptures, for us to gnaw on.

Nor need we limit ourselves to the Scriptures. Mankind, in its thousands of years of practical experience with the realities of life, has made countless discoveries of the sort of behavior that leads to fulfillment, and of other sorts that may, at the outset, look good, but that prove in the end self-defeating.

Why ignore this body of wisdom? It is vast. And is it any less scientific than the discoveries of chemistry, merely because its findings weren't precipitated in test tubes?

There is another, and perfectly valid, kind of "laboratory": that of human experience. What this laboratory

39

lacks in measured precision, when compared to the physical sciences, it more than makes up for in another vital criterion of those sciences: usefulness to mankind.

A person who takes up the sword may in fact not *always* perish by the sword. Many who have perished, moreover, might actually have saved themselves from death had they possessed weapons of some sort. Jesus' statement, then, may lack scientific precision. But it is nevertheless a practical guideline to the difference between using force to obtain what one wants, and attaining one's ends by the consent and with the cooperation of others. Anything that is wrested from others by violence is likely to awaken in them a desire to wrest it back again just as violently.

Science, too, has its dogmas, and protects them as jealously as any church. The modern scientific era began with a search for provable physical realities. Science thus limited its search to such relatively simple questions as those pertaining to mass, weight, and motion.

Now, however, even psychological and spiritual realities tend to be viewed with a materialistic bias. As much as possible, they are even tested in material terms. This approach is like trying to explain the ascendency of one artist over others purely in terms of his physical weight, or of the speed with which he can move his brush over a canvas.

The centuries have given us many useful axioms for how to get what we want from life. Some of these may seem contrary to common sense. What justifies them, ultimately, is the fact that they work.

For example, in every age, and in virtually every culture, mankind has been warned against selfishness. Why? It seems the most obvious truism in the world that everyone is more interested in his own happiness than in that of others. Why pretend otherwise? To put it bluntly, why *shouldn't* we get out there with hammer and tong (or sickle) and "get ours"? Common sense militates against unselfishness as a virtue, regardless of what the ages have to say on the subject.

Why not, indeed, *rob* others of their happiness to increase our own?

The answer, if submitted to actual testing in the "laboratory" of human experience, begins with the simple observation that selfish people are never happy—or not, certainly, in those aspects of their lives in which they are selfish.

The second observation is that unselfish persons *are* happy—again, at least in those aspects of their lives in which they are unselfish.

Even murderers have been known to be kind to animals, and to be happy at least in those relationships. But unrepentant murderers are not, on the whole, notably happy people.

The ancient warning not to be selfish is based, not on someone's self-interest in getting others to be generous to *him,* but on thousands of years of observation on the part of wise people who have studied how to help man to achieve the fulfillment he himself wants from life.

Again, this observation, like experiments in the chemist's laboratory, is repeatable. Nowhere do we hear of any authority saying, "I tried what they said about selfishness vs. generosity, and I found they were wrong. Selfishness alone, not generosity, is what works."

Oh, indeed, we may read a Jean Paul Sartre—or an Ayn Rand—*claiming* that egocentricity is the answer. But do we find it really working, either in their own lives or in the lives of others? Not at all. All the wisdom of the ages is weighted on the side of selflessness.

The next question would be, Why has this been so? And the explanation would be found in John Donne's statement, "No man is an island." We are, all of us, parts of a greater reality. No man can be happy who, denying this greater reality, confines his identity to the suffocating prison of a little ego.

This explanation is supported by a further, and well tested, observation: that any expansion of self-identity is rewarding, whereas any contraction of self-identity is one of the primary causes of pain.

There is no need for pious platitudes in the realm of human behavior, any more than there is room for wishful thinking in experiments with the behavior of laboratory animals.

Consider a scientist experimenting with the learning ability of rats. He wants them to find their way through a complex maze. Accordingly, at the end of every wrong turn he sets an electric wire which provides a slight shock to any rat as yet so unschooled as to run into it. At the end of the correct series of turns, however, will be placed a bit of food.

Punishment—and reward. When a rat is punished for doing what the experimenter doesn't want it to do, and rewarded for doing what it is supposed to do, it soon learns how to behave in that context because, as it discovers at last, the right choices give it what it itself wants.

Even worms have been taught to do likewise, with simpler choices.

This, then, is an approach that can be taken in the classroom, if we would teach our children once more a set of fundamental moral standards. The issue is not sectarian, dogmatic, or sentimental. It is simply that wise persons throughout the ages have claimed, and history has substantiated, that certain kinds of behavior work *for* mankind, whereas other kinds work *against* humanity's true interests.

Children should be invited to test these claims by their own experience. But there is no need to leave them to discover their truth all by themselves, any more than one would expect them to rediscover the rules of algebra, or to reinvent the wheel. It isn't dogmatizing them to say to them, "These principles work," if one explains how they work, and why, and particularly if one invites them to test these principles for themselves.

Why, indeed, be honest, and not dishonest? Truthful, rather than untruthful? Self-controlled, rather than self-abandoned? Concentrated, rather than scattered? Kind, rather than callous? Cooperative, rather than over-competitive? Why? Simply because, in the long run, right action alone really serves mankind, whereas wrong action invariably disappoints one in the end.

And that, of course, is what makes it wrong in the first place.

7

To What End?

A WOMAN OF MY ACQUAINTANCE one day, in an effort to break her two-year-old child of certain infantile habits, said to him, "Come on now, you're not a baby any longer."

The little boy looked up at her with a happy smile and replied, "But I *like* being a baby!"

Another friend once was asked by her five-year-old daughter, "Mommy, what do you think about during the day."

"Well," the mother replied, "I think about you children, and about Daddy, and about our friends."

"I don't," rejoined the little girl seriously. "I think about me." After a pause she continued thoughtfully, "Why do little children think about themselves?"

Interesting conversations, both of them.

We assume that children have a *desire* to grow up. But even adults are prone to resist change. How much more so, then, babies, secure in the loving embrace of their mothers; or little children, more interested in themselves than in the world— what to speak of the vast universe?—around them.

And yet, even at such a young age my friend's little daughter was able also to universalize her self-preoccupation, to expand her identity to include all other children. There is an inclination on the part of children not only to cling to what they already know, but also to enlarge their horizons.

Indeed, expansion is instinctive to life itself. The important thing to understand, especially where children are concerned, is that they need to be *invited* toward maturity. The ever-expanding vision of reality that they will be given during the process of growing up must be introduced to them sensitively. Otherwise, instead of attracting them, it will repel.

Even adults may feel themselves threatened by challenges too far beyond any they have so far contemplated. I well remember an experience I myself have had in this connection.

Of the diverse activities that may engage a person during his lifetime, my own have happened to include the founding of a community. This village, in fact, over nearly twenty years of struggles and challenges, has managed to grow, and even to flourish. But when it was new—as often happens with starting projects—it showed few outward signs of success.

Sometimes, in those days, I would share with others my dreams for the community's future. My intention was to inspire. To my astonishment, however, many found this vision of the future threatening. They needed to take our development a step at a time. Gradually, as they did so over the years they found themselves able to grow into things naturally and happily.

I mentioned in the last chapter that some of the principles of right behavior are so far from being obvious as to seem contrary to common sense. I gave as an example the virtually universal precept against selfishness. Well, if such teachings defy common sense in adults, how can we expect children to embrace them?

One even wonders whether our little ones don't sometimes feel themselves lost in a wilderness of adult values.

A cousin of mine, as a child, was always getting into scrapes. He was physically strong, and usually came out the victor. One afternoon, when he'd returned home with a torn shirt, his mother admonished him, "Don't you know, dear, that when someone hits you, you shouldn't hit back?"

"Oh, but Mother," the boy replied self-righteously, "I never hit back. I *always* hit first!"

It isn't easy to teach children values, when their vision of things is often so different from our own. How can we win them to a maturity that includes others' realities in their own? Precepts that can be taught to an adult are often difficult to explain to a child. In fact, let us face it, even adults don't always have an easy time with them.

Our task is to attract children toward maturity—that is, toward an attitude that includes others' realities in their own. A child has a strong need for security within his present boundaries. Fortunately, he feels at the same time a need steadily to expand those boundaries, as he senses in himself the capability to push them progressively outward.

Many of the fantasies of childhood, for example, though perhaps foolish in the eyes of literal-minded adults, are important to children. A child needs to be taken step by step, and not in one giant leap, toward an understanding of things as they really are. For one thing, if he is brought sensitively to maturity, he will not lose the priceless gift of imagination, without which no great achievements in life are possible.

Again, a child needs to know what his limits are, and can't be happy if he is given no guidelines. To be told, "No, you may *not* cross the street unattended," may invoke in him an uncomprehending rage, but it is a necessary guideline nevertheless, and the very firmness of the limits it imposes will give him a certain sense of security.

The child must be allowed to expand his vision of things at his own pace. He should be ever encouraged, but never forced, in this direction by his adult mentors.

It would help, however, to find, among all the precepts he is expected to learn during the process of growing up, *one single* explanation for them that he will recognize as a constant, and that will reassure him with a sense of the familiar every time some new precept is presented for his consideration.

He may not quickly understand the need, for example, to include others' realities in his own. He may not easily relate to the benefits, to him, of being generous to others. He may be merely bewildered by the—again, to him—incredible suggestion that, when hit, he shouldn't hit back. And in teaching him each of these precepts, it may be difficult to get him to memorize them, presented as they might be separately, and without any relation to one another.

Is there some simple, single reason why a child should be good: a sort of "Unified Field Theory" in human behavior? one that will avoid that common, but perhaps simplistic, explanation, "If you don't behave, you'll get a walloping!"?

Yes, in fact there is. There is an explanation that can serve equally well at every stage on the long journey toward true maturity.

47

For, regardless of any other motivation, there is in all human striving *one over-riding consideration.* It can be applied with even greater effectiveness to the child than to the adult. For the child's basic motivations are less concealed by a fog of extraneous considerations: "What will the neighbors think? Will behaving this way toward my family help me outside the home, in my career? Will friendliness to the customers win me points with the boss?" The child's motivations, in other words, are not so likely to be confused by ulterior motives.

What do people *really* want, at the heart of all their multifarious activities? Quite simply, *they want to escape pain, and to find happiness.*

Why, for example, do they seek employment? First, because they want to escape the pain of hunger and financial insecurity. And second, because they want to find happiness—whether in the work itself, or through the opportunities for enjoyment that are afforded by a steady income.

Why do people climb mountains? Is it only, as Hillary claimed, "to get to the top"? Why would anyone *want* to get to the top? Quite simply, because the climber has it in his mind that at the top, for him, lies some kind of fulfillment, which is to say, happiness.

And why do people resort to collecting—as a recent bulk mailing invited me to do—"artistic replicas," in silver, of emblems on the hoods of automobiles in the early nineteen-twenties? All, to escape what for some, one assumes, must be the intolerable pain of not owning such a collection, and to attain the sheer ecstasy of possessing one. It all depends on what desires you harbor in your heart.

"Le monde," as the French say, *"où l'on s'amuse."*

Underneath all the variety of human desires, however, there are certain types of behavior that, for everyone, have the same basic value. Whether or not you climb mountains, or collect emblems, is of course a matter of taste. But it is never a matter of taste when it comes to kindness vs. cruelty; generosity vs. selfishness; calmness vs. nervousness; cheerfulness, and other positive attitudes, vs. negativity and moodiness; sharing credit vs. claiming all the credit for oneself.

Whatever the human value under discussion, the issues can be explained with perfect clarity in these simple, but most fundamental, terms: *By right behavior, the child will avoid pain to himself, and (even more important) will increase his own happiness.*

8

Education for Life in the Classroom

Sir ROY REDGRAVE, former Commander of the British armed forces in the Far East, once remarked to me, "The character of every regiment is determined by its leadership."

The same is true of businesses, of monasteries—of any activity where groups of people are involved. The spirit of the leader, or leaders, determines both the character and the spirit of a group. Hence, the importance of developing leadership in those who show a talent for it.

And hence also the importance, to schools, of developing teachers. For if children are to be taught according to this new system, which I have called "Education for Life," it is imperative that their teachers first be trained in it. Otherwise, their old, customary teaching methods will in time reassert themselves.

To teach the principles here outlined, special classes will have to be developed in the schools. And for these above all, special teacher training will be necessary.

There is much also, however, that might be done with conventional subjects to impart the basic principles of an "Education for Life." The important thing here would be to see these principles, not as an intrusion on established subjects, but as central to the teaching of those subjects.

Here, then, arc a few suggestions for how this end might be achieved—suggestions which, in turn, might help spark other creative ideas in teachers' minds.

History teachers, for example, might make it a point not to teach history only as a series of past events, but as a present guideline—personal for the students, as well as objectively useful.

I referred in an earlier chapter to the Battle of Agincourt. Let us consider that event, therefore, as an example of the kind of teaching I am describing.

In 1415 A.D., King Henry V of England, against seemingly impossible odds, vanquished the flower of French chivalry by introducing a new method of warfare. His technique was to rely primarily on his foot soldiers and on the English longbow.

Another battle, similar in its recourse to unusual tactics by the weaker force, was fought during the middle ages by Swiss peasants against their noble overlords. The peasants had, as weapons, only scythes and pitchforks. The noblemen were heavily armored, and on horseback.

What the peasants did was flood the battlefield with water on the eve of battle. It was the dead of winter, and the water froze overnight. When their lordly enemies sallied forth on the following morning, both horses and men were rendered utterly helpless, slipping and falling all over the ice. The peasants came onto the ice properly shod, and dispatched the lot of them.

What practical lessons might children learn from these, and similar, examples in history? Well, for one thing, that solutions to problems often come from being solution-oriented, rather than problem-oriented; that opposite cases—history's great failures—often resulted from people brooding on the hopelessness of their predicament, instead of looking confidently for a way out of it.

Children might learn also that creative initiative can accomplish far more than brute force; and determined energy, more than complacent power.

Again, they might learn that tradition-honored ways of doing things are not always the best, and that a fresh and better approach usually requires pulling back a little bit, mentally, and consciously looking for it.

History is full of examples that can be turned, similarly, to good advantage. And wouldn't it be vastly more enjoyable to learn, and for that matter to teach it, that way? What matter if a few uninteresting dates, irrelevant events, and insignificant individuals receive less, or even no, mention for lack of the usual time devoted to them? One must in any case be selective in one's teaching, when spanning the centuries. Why not, then, select with greater attention to the students' real needs?

*   *   *

Consider foreign languages.

It might be helpful, to start with, to offer a new academic course: an overview of general linguistic trends. Such a course would include a study of how languages evolve; of basic differences between one language and another; of where words come from; and of how our use of words directs our way of thinking.

Take, for example, the Romance languages. These, unlike English, assign a gender to every noun. When you start a sentence in French or Italian, you must be already committed to whatever nouns you intend to use, for only by knowing in advance whether they are masculine or feminine can you know what modifying words to start out with.

When speaking French, for example, one is forced to be conscious not only of concepts, but of the words he uses to express those concepts. The advantages, but also the disadvantages, of such rigidly logical expression force themselves also on the way people in the Latin countries think.

English, in this sense, is a more intuitive language. You can "switch horses" in the midstream of an English sentence, selecting at a moment's notice, perhaps, some word that you hadn't at first thought to use, but that you now see better suits your purpose.

The ultimate purpose of this sort of study is that it makes the student more mentally flexible, more aware of other ways of thinking and of seeing things. Respect for another person's mental processes is part of what it means to be mature—to be aware of, and thus to relate, to *his* realities, and not only to one's own.

The point, however, of any system of "Education for Life" is not only to draw morals from the things one teaches. Too much moralizing, indeed, can become hopelessly dreary, even if the goal of it all is to guide the student toward his own self-fulfillment. But one of the greatest lessons that life can teach is how to *enjoy* whatever one does—and, in the classroom, to enjoy whatever one teaches, or learns.

In this respect, conventional pedagogy, rooted as it is in

the transmission of a fixed body of knowledge, tends to become sterile. The learning process ought to be rooted in life itself, and therefore—for the teacher just as much as for the student—a thing daily fresh and wonderful. Any teacher who really *enjoys* what he teaches, and who can spark a kindred enjoyment in his students, has already mastered one of the central points in an "Education for Life."

If conventional teaching sparks few creative references to their own lives in the students' minds, it is because facts, by themselves, are static and immutable. Too much devotion to committing facts to memory actually discourages the fluidity and dynamism of creative thought. Teachers themselves, if they teach by this method, tend to sink into a rut from which they end up resenting any effort to dislodge them.

The very examples they use in their teaching often reveal an extraordinary lack of imagination.

We were discussing the teaching of languages. A rather stuffy book of guidelines that I once saw for the English-speaking tourist in Germany offered this helpful German sentence: "Stop, barber, you have put the brush in my mouth!"

Most of us have also been through the dry declensions of nouns, the "amo-amas-amatting" of verbs, the presentation of even living languages as though they were dead and mummified.

I once saw a cartoon in The New Yorker magazine: a sign in a Paris shop that read, "College French spoken here."

In my own experience, I recall getting low marks in a course in French, even though, having spent a year and a half as a boy in a school in French Switzerland, I spoke the language relatively well. In fact, my teacher admitted that I spoke it better than he did. But I'd learned it by speaking it. It was difficult for me to relate this living language to the lifeless lists we'd been given to memorize in the classroom.

Why not include in the study of languages a study also of the people who speak them, their history, their national characteristics, their heroes? Why not study language, in other words, *from the inside out?*

If, for example, the subject is Italian, it will help enormously to identify, from the heart, with the Italian people, and not to look upon them as "those crazy people, with their weird manner of speech." That is what Italians and their noble language are likely to remain for the student, if all he learns in the classroom is lists of verb forms, and stilted sentences like, "My tailor is good."

I myself began the study of Italian in my fifties, which is generally considered to be too late in life to learn a new language. Yet, by following the method of creative involvement suggested here, I became able within a relatively short time not only to converse, but even to lecture in Italian. I have, on occasion, actually been mistaken for an Italian—in Italy.

From the standpoint of an "Education for Life," there is much to be gained from learning to approach *any* new subject as it were *from within*—from its core, rather than from its periphery. And one way to accomplish that is to involve one's students totally in any subject they study.

And what matter if, in the process, traditional teaching lines have to be crossed? For a language teacher to teach a little of Italy's history along with its language may constitute a minor incursion into the history teacher's domain, but where is the harm in getting the student to see the same history from a second point of view?

Indeed, it is partly in the rigid compartmentalizing of its subjects that formal education loses so much of its potential relevance. Compartmentalized knowledge rather resembles an approach to the study of the human body by examining the head alone, then the lungs alone, then the intestines, and so forth, while ignoring the living interrelationship of the different parts to one another.

* * *

In the study of mathematics, then, considerable interest in the subject might be sparked by including in the course a general history of mathematics. Interesting, too, would be a study of the lives of great mathematicians, and perhaps of the challenges they faced in getting their work accepted.

Great mathematicians often have a sense of the sheer poetry of numbers—a sense that is seldom hinted at, perhaps not even imagined, by most teachers of math courses.

There is Pythagoras's application of mathematics to the study of music: a fascinating subject, but one rarely mentioned in the classroom.

Of great and practical interest to students of algebra would be a study of the importance of symbolic logic in everyday life—of making a definition serve in place of a complex reality as a means of simplifying thought. The advantages, and also the disadvantages, of symbolic thinking make a fascinating and important study.

For we engage in it all the time, consciously or unconsciously, and on many levels of our lives. There is, for example, symbolic thinking on an emotional level, where a person will say one thing while meaning another, and expect to be understood. There is the symbolism of poetry, with its use of rain, for instance, to imply sorrow, or the flowers of spring to suggest new beginnings. And there is the importance of learning to distinguish between symbolic and literal thought—the importance, in other words, of learning not to confuse definition with reality.

Children in the lower grades, on the other hand, could have emphasized to them, when faced with arithmetic's immutable realities, the importance of accepting and adapting to things *as they are.* Two plus two always makes four; it is not a matter of whim. The children may have been used to getting their own way in certain things, but here is an example, selected from countless realities in life, of something that no amount of wishing can change.

There is even something that might be taught—a point, incidentally, of considerable interest: that different types of human activity require different directions of energy. Language or music, for example, require a greater focus of energy in the heart. Mathematics and logic require, if one is to master them, a more abstract consciousness, a state of mind that may be aided, as the yogis of India suggest, by focusing one's thoughts at a point midway between the eyebrows.

And, again, the mastery of any subject requires that one identify himself with the particular state of consciousness for which that subject holds an affinity.

* * *

Nor, for younger children, should the importance of fantasy be overlooked. History, for example, could be taught them as seen through the eyes of a little boy and girl traveling backwards in a time machine to ages long past, and relating what they see to their own lives today.

Geography, again, might be taught as seen through the eyes of a boy and girl traveling to distant places, and experiencing those places in terms of their own immediate realities.

In every field, even the most prosaic, there are endless opportunities for creative application of these "Education for Life" principles.

9

The Importance of Experience

Much CAN BE DONE in the teaching of conventional subjects to educate children in the art of living. In order seriously to offer them an "Education for Life," however, special training in this art needs to be offered as well, both in separate classes and outside the classroom.

An intellectual understanding of how to live is never sufficient. Even in so intellectual a subject as algebra, John Saxon, a teacher famous for the efficacy of his methods, has demonstrated the importance of grounding students in constant practice.

Saxon has convinced many teachers of the appeal, moreover, of humor, and of offering down-to-earth, human situations when presenting a problem. In his book, *Algebra I,* he wrote: "At the Mardi Gras ball, the guests roistered and rollicked until the wee hours. If the ratio of roisterers to rollickers was 7 to 5 and 1080 were in attendance, how many were rollickers?" Students find this sort of problem much more fun to consider than, let us say, the ratio of trucks to wheelbarrows filled with cement. Math problems are commonly stated with no thought at all to giving the students a good time. It is almost like the notorious "Protestant ethic": "If you enjoy it, it can't be good for you."

If in conventional studies there is a need for experience, in the sense of repeated practice, and not only for intellectual exposure—a point hotly contested, incidentally, by the majority of Saxon's peers in the school system—how self-evidently is it true for the living values that are the focus of this book.

Well, on second thought, perhaps it is too sanguine to call it self-evident. For we live today in a society that holds practically as a dogma the notion that to define a thing is to understand it. All teaching, virtually, is of the blackboard variety.

Many a psychiatrist, even, sees it as his duty merely to get a patient to "see" his point. "Yes, Doc, it's true, I do hate my father. Thank you for telling me it's o.k. to do so." Or, "Yes, Doc, I see that my problem is insecurity and a low self-image." The patient may even be brought to the point of realizing that he needs to give more emotional support to his father, and to rely less on his parent's approval in return. But even at this point, how much has been really accomplished, except intellectually?

I have known many highly intelligent people to pride themselves on the range and subtlety of their self-understanding, while never taking a single step toward actual self-reformation. It is as though, by mental acceptance of the need for making an inner change, they somehow imagined that the change had already been made!

The more intelligent a person, it often seems, the more difficult it is for him seriously to commit himself to positive action.

Of course, I am not referring to intelligence *per se*. The greatest deeds in any field of endeavor are always performed by people with a high degree of intelligence. My reference, rather, is to those whose intelligence is, in a manner of speaking, ingrown; whose intellectuality tends to isolate them from objective reality, or to content them with merely reading about reality.

Such, indeed, as I have already said, is the weakness of too much intellectuality, and consequently of our modern educational system. The very people who are the most involved with the system—the teachers and professors—are usually those who are the most opposed to change of any kind. Their intellectual bias is toward theorizing, and toward a corresponding lack of practical commitment.

Much can be accomplished toward giving children an "Education for Life," even during the process of teaching standard classroom subjects. Special classes, however, in the art of living need to be taught also, filled with narrative examples, practical illustrations, and useful techniques that the children themselves can practice both in the classroom and at home.

There need to be classes in self-expression; in understanding oneself and others; in cooperation with others; in the true meaning of success; in how to succeed; in how to exert a positive influence on others; in joyful self-discipline, and in the importance of right, positive attitudes; in the art of concentration; in developing memory; in general problem solving; in secrets of achieving true happiness. The list given here is by no means exhaustive, but is intended to suggest a direction that, if pursued, will open up ever fresh channels of its own. Suffice it that the classes be *living,* not didactic.

Outside the classroom, time should be set apart also for

a more spontaneous, more individualized type of education. In this respect it is a pity that most education is only a daytime affair. Far more can be accomplished with students who live at school full time during the school months.

Paramhansa Yogananda, the spiritual leader and teacher, when directing a boys' boarding school in Ranchi, India, had two students who were bitter enemies. Counseling them proved a failure, so he had them sleep together in the same bed. From then on it was either constant warfare, or grudging peace. After some struggle, they decided on peace. And gradually they became friends.

After some time, Yogananda decided really to force the lesson home to them. Standing at the head of their bed while they slept, he reached down carefully and rapped one of them on the forehead.

The boy rose up wrathfully, accusing his bedmate of breaking the peace.

"I didn't hit you, I swear it!" cried the other, wide-eyed with surprise.

Both settled back to sleep. Minutes later, Yogananda rapped the other boy on the forehead.

"I told you I didn't do it!" cried the boy furiously. They were about to join in battle when they saw their teacher smiling down at them.

"Oh," they cried in amazement. *"You!"*

This shared episode, and the humorous light that it cast on their previous enmity, cemented their friendship from that time onward.

I grant that this sort of teaching demands both the right occasion and the right teacher. The limitations imposed by daytime education make such in-depth training all the more difficult. And the difficulty of finding wise teachers makes teacher training, and a greater appreciation on the part of society for the role of teachers, imperative.

Meanwhile, what can be accomplished with things as they are?

It is difficult to avoid artificiality, when seeking to give anyone actual experience in even the most common living situations. The very act of saying, "Now we shall experience how and why to forgive others," not only creates a false situation, but also encourages superficial responses to it.

Obviously, then, teachers need to be aware of, and quickly responsive to, situations as they actually arise in the lives of their students. The test of a teacher's wisdom will lie in his ability to recognize a problem, and to respond to it sensitively and appropriately. For instance, were a teacher to leap enthusiastically at every opportunity to instruct his students in the art of living the moment such an opportunity presents itself, he might well develop in them, eventually, a resentment against all instruction in human values.

I knew a teacher who suffered from this excess of zeal. A girl in his class one day suffered an accident with her bicycle, and was lying, weeping, in the school driveway. The teacher, coming and crouching over her, demanded, "Now, Nancy, analyze your thoughts. *Why* did you have this accident? Be honest with yourself. You're trying to escape something, aren't you? Can't you see that you've *attracted* what's happened?"

Poor child! All she needed at that point was a little

comfort. And if her need sprang, on some inner level, from self-deception, what of it? Love a child when he weeps, and he may be the more ready to listen to reason once he's calm again. And maybe it isn't really reason he needs anyway.

It is difficult enough to deal wisely with living situations. It is far more difficult to create them artificially, for the purposes of instruction.

Much, however, can be accomplished by a sort of deliberate artificiality, in the form of fantasy: stories acted out; little dramatic pieces; story reading that involves the children's response and verbal participation.

In this respect, an excellent lesson can be taken from the children themselves. For what is the universal game played by children everywhere, regardless of culture or nationality? Let's pretend:

"You, Johnny, be the dragon. Jeannie, you be the princess. And I'll be the prince who comes to the castle to save her, riding a white horse and wearing a shiny sword."

Best of all, then, would be games of *Let's Pretend.*

"Here is the dragon. He was once a soldier who wanted to protect his princess. One day, he fought off the attack of an evil wizard who wanted to carry the princess off to his dungeon. The wizard therefore cursed him to become a dragon, and as well to assume a dragon's violent nature.

"Now the dragon will never let any man near his princess, and is doomed to lay waste the countryside for miles around with his fiery breath. No man can destroy him, no matter how sharp or shiny his sword.

"If any man can *forgive* him, however, deeply, from his heart, his forgiveness will break the evil spell cast by the wizard's vengeful spirit. By forgiveness, the dragon will be turned back into a good and loyal soldier. And the brave knight who saved him will marry the princess."

An important point to be realized, when helping children to achieve fresh insight into the problems they encounter in daily life, is that the intellectual understanding of a problem, far from being insufficient, is often not even helpful. What *is* important is that they find themselves moving happily in a new direction, and not that they understand all the reasons for this new direction.

I am reminded here of a story from the life of St. Francis of Assisi. St. Francis and a small group of his friars minor were walking one day along a country road, and singing joyfully of God's love. At a certain turn, a stranger approached them, and threw himself on his knees before Francis, begging to be admitted as a disciple. St. Francis lovingly accepted him.

Brother Elias, as this man came to be called, joined the friars on their walk. He was really more a scholar than a saint. In fact, he was not really, at heart, even a friar. In later years, he was to become the general of the Franciscan Order, from which time onward his analytical nature would undermine much of the spontaneous, free spirit that marked the Order during this early period of its history.

This day, however, he merely spoke to the others as they strolled along, and explained his reasons for joining the Order, and the importance of the Order to all of mankind.

The merry friars had been walking along, singing. Now, suddenly, the impulse of song died in their hearts. They continued their walk in an uneasy silence.

Who would want to kill the song in a child's heart? Instead of explaining to him the benefits of living harmoniously, why not get him simply to do things that are harmonious? That very act will help to lift him into a habitually positive frame of mind.

Singing, too, is a wonderful therapy. No need to explain why it is, to the child. Just get him to sing happy songs. You will find in music one of the best ways of bringing out the best in him.

Dance is another excellent form of therapy. Body movements are closely allied to attitudes of the mind.

It might also help to get children to make affirmations while moving their bodies.

They can walk vigorously in place, for example, affirming as they do so, "I am awake and ready!"

They can stretch their arms out sidewise, in front, and above their heads, affirming, "I am positive, energetic, enthusiastic!"

They can rub the palms of their hands vigorously over their bodies, crying, "Awake! Rejoice, my body cells!"

And they can rub their heads lightly with their finger tips, repeating, "Be glad, my brain! Be wise and strong!"

They can use the centering movements of dance to affirm, "I live ever peacefully at the heart of my being."

Certain outward-reaching movements of dance might be used to affirm, "I reach out in love to serve all my fellow creatures."

Upward-reaching movements might be accompanied by the affirmation, "I reach up to the highest that is in me."

Downward gestures could accompany the affirmation: "I reach downward to uplift all those who weep."

Vigorous dance steps and gestures might be accompanied by the words, "Troubles may threaten, but I conquer all."

Certain yoga postures, with related affirmations, are notably calming and invigorating also.

Painting, too, can be a means of drawing out feelings in a child which, once objectified, might be emphasized, if they are constructive, or positively redirected, if they are not.

Any shared activity, moreover, whether of play, games, or work, can be a means of harnessing excess energy and directing it in a positive way.

A final word: Never underestimate the importance of fun to the over-all teaching process. It is often during moments of relaxation that the most fundamental lessons are learned.

10

True Education Is Self-Education

IT HAS BEEN WELL SAID that a truth cannot be learned: it can only be recognized.

As I stated earlier, it isn't realistic to ask a child to determine what he shall learn. Mature decisions cannot be made in ignorance of the facts. But this much having been said, it remains equally true that unless the child also *wants* to learn, no amount of teaching will force him to absorb anything. Effective teaching requires the student's willing cooperation, and this willingness must be enlisted; it cannot be commandeered.

Thus, whatever the system of education, it must be flexible enough to provide for the shifting needs of a large variety of students. *It must be child-oriented, not teacher-oriented.* A teacher may have specific information that he wants to share, but if his students are not ready to receive it, his immediate job must be either to help make them ready, or else to concentrate on teaching them what he thinks they *can* learn.

One of the mistakes often made by teachers and lecturers is the tendency to speak to impress themselves, rather than to benefit their audiences. But a good class or lecture is dialogue, even if only one person does the speaking. The competent speaker will "listen" intuitively to the unspoken questions of his audience, and perhaps even to their unconscious needs, and will respond accordingly. The more intuitive he is, the greater will be his ability to sense his listeners' overall needs, and even the needs of individual members of his audience.

On the general level, groups of people often share a kind of awareness to which the sensitive lecturer can respond, if he will but "listen" in his heart. In such cases it often happens that, the larger the group, the stronger its shared awareness. I have found that in lecturing to 2,000 people there may actually be a greater sense of dialogue than when lecturing to only six persons.

The attention of older children, similarly, can be enlisted relatively easily in groups. It isn't necessary in the classroom, except sporadically, to address them individually. They, unlike little children, can be interested on a level of principles, and don't require a constant reference to personalities in order to hold their attention.

With younger children, however—because they are less comfortable with abstract principles—this practice of "listening" to one's listeners may demand a much more literal application.

Especially during the early years of education, close attention should be given to every child. Classes should be small, if possible. Care should be taken to observe the child's reactions, and to note how best to enlist his interest and willing cooperation individually.

Some children are more physically oriented; others, more emotionally; still others, more mentally. Some can be stimulated by a challenge to their will power; and others, by an appeal to their finer feelings. Some must have the logic of a request pointed out to them. Still others will respond only to firm orders.

I remember my father once spanking my brother Bob and me for something we'd done wrong—wrong, at least, in his adult eyes. As we children saw it, we'd contributed our responsible bit to the beautification of the bathroom, by scratching stars on its newly painted walls.

Bob, whose orientation was more physical than mine, accepted the spanking as part of the natural order of things, and promptly forgot all about it. But my outlook was primarily mental. A physical spanking for what had been, after all, my best of intentions seemed to me an outrage against higher justice.

Weeks later, I looked at my father accusingly and demanded, "Why did you spank me?" He in turn, recognizing that the spanking had been a mistake, never spanked me again.

It would be helpful to prepare a file on every child, listing his salient characteristics, his reactions to discipline, or to instruction, and suggesting directions that might be taken in his own personal "Education for Life."

It is probable that the child will fall naturally into one or another of the four types suggested above: physical, emotional, will power, or intellect.

Certain contrasts might be considered also. Is he by nature expansive, or contractive? outgoing, or withdrawn? positive, or negative? constructive, or destructive? imaginative, or literal? creative, or imitative? aggressive, or passive? assertive, or submissive?

It is generally assumed that it is better for a child, in each of these cases, to be the first of the pair, not the second. An extroverted child, for example, is considered better adjusted than one who is introverted. But this is simplistic. Adjusted to *what?* To himself, merely because he is not sufficiently introspective to be aware of his own shortcomings? To the society around him? It is often to the introvert that people turn for meaningful communication. Creative geniuses too, moreover, are often introverted. And who will lament the presence of geniuses in our midst?

In many of the pairs mentioned above, the second is not a defect. Nor is it one to be transformed at all costs into its opposite quality. It may become rather a virtue, once it has been refined, and its potentials fully explored.

Submissiveness, for example, may be developed more easily than over-aggressiveness into the positive trait of willing cooperation.

A literal mentality may never be inspired to create works of imaginative genius, but it may easily become interested in the more pragmatic sciences. Thus, a tendency toward literalness, in some contexts a defect, might in other contexts be developed into a virtue.

In all cases, it is important to work *with* the child's strengths, rather than *on* his weaknesses. Usually, he will respond far better to this positive approach.

To clarify the direction in which a child's character may be developed, it must be realized that there are various levels of refinement in human nature. In some applications, this statement will seem obvious enough. Negativity and destructiveness, for example, are undesirable traits both in society and in the child himself, and no effort should be spared to rechannel such energies in a more positive direction. But for many qualities, it is not easy to discern the direction of progressive refinement.

An obstacle to the very exercise of such discernment is one of the fundamental tenets of modern education.

Tenet? Call it, rather, a dogma. There is today the peculiar conviction, one that is challenged at one's peril, that human beings are born equal in all their native abilities. Surely, the well-known dictum, "All men are created equal," cannot have been intended so literally.

It is one thing to say that all men are created equal before God; or that, in their shared humanity, all have equally the right to rise to their own levels of competence, to develop their own talents, and to fulfill their reasonable desires according to their own intrinsic abilities.

It may even be justifiable, philosophically speaking, to say that all men have the *potential* to attain to equal heights.

It is quite another thing, however, to say that all men are *already* equally competent, equally talented, and equally capable of achieving success. Any fool can see that they are not. How is it that intelligent people can so blind themselves to the obvious? Only a person exceptionally steeped in the practice of substituting theory for reality, surely, can even contemplate such a possibility.

Worse than the error itself—after all, we do all make mistakes—is the evil that the error has produced: the widespread envy that is so much the hallmark of contemporary social thinking.

Can you even count the number of times you've heard the boast: "I'm just as good as anyone else."

Good at *what?* Or do the people who make this boast

mean, simply, *good?* That is, do they consider themselves as virtuous as any saint, and possessed of no traits which might be improved? Is the only reason others have achieved greater success in life than they, or greater popularity, or more widespread influence, simply that they themselves never had the opportunities others did, or that Certain People—envious, perhaps, of their sterling worth—withheld those opportunities from them deliberately?

What foolishness!

And yet, the people who subscribe to this folly are legion. They are responsible for much of the anger and violence of our Twentieth Century.

In the classrooms, the equation of equality with uniformity has led to the careful nurturing of mediocrity.

Teaching is geared, supposedly, to the average student. (In this sense a sop is thrown, though hardly respectfully, to the principle of "listening" to the students.) The very decision to focus on the average involves a *downward* direction of energy. (No one ever thinks of *raising* the quality of teaching to the average level.) Thus, once reaching down to the average level is established as the norm, the tendency is to continue to reach down further still, in order to gather in the somewhat less-than-average student.

A downward direction having been well established, indeed, many teachers end up devoting most of their attention to their dullest students. Necessarily, in the process, the quality of instruction becomes diminished to the point of being bastardized.

Meanwhile, the brilliant students' abilities receive few, or no, real challenges. These students soon become bored.

Often, indeed, it is these who end up becoming "problem" children in the schools.

And what is the result of this system? Modern education prepares people well enough for reading the newspaper, but it leaves them more or less at a loss when confronted with Shakespeare.

Intelligence is only one standard of a student's all-round qualifications. But it is obvious that all students are not equally intelligent. And from this self-evident fact it should follow fairly smoothly that neither are they equally sensitive, creative, receptive, energetic, willing, or, in fact, equally *anything.* In a world where no two thumbprints are alike, how much greater is the variety in human capabilities.

Can we point, then, to progressive *levels* of development, of refinement, in these capabilities? In the case of intelligence, such a progression is more or less discernible. But what of other qualities of human nature?

The question needs to be approached from the standpoint of human nature itself. What does this nature itself demand for its fulfillment?

I've already mentioned the universal need to escape pain and achieve happiness. This is a general criterion. But now that we've introduced the concept of progressive development, further criteria need to be introduced. In our consideration of these criteria, it must be remembered that their focus is on the child's own self-development—that is to say, on the particular. Only from there may we proceed to the universal.

But enough of theories that need no regular watering with facts, simply because they're completely artificial!

11

Progressive Development

A FRIEND OF MINE one day, struggling in the quicksands of a negative mood, was attempting to define everything in life in terms of the general hopelessness of it all. He challenged me to say something that would make him see things differently. And of course, my best efforts proved unavailing. For when a person *wants* to be unhappy, no one in the world can make him happy.

But then an inspiration came to me. "I'm not really worried about you," I said. "Each of us has his own specific spiritual gravity, and returns to it again and again during the relaxation that follows any period of depression or euphoria. Your own specific gravity is high. I'm sure you'll return to it effortlessly in a day or two, without any help from me."

And so indeed it proved.

It was an interesting thought. Objects of varying specific gravity sink, as everybody knows, to different depths in a body of water. But people, too, sink or rise in consciousness, according to a kind of specific mental gravity. Some are more naturally heavy; others, more naturally light.

People with a naturally positive outlook will rise, even in the face of extraordinary set-backs: tests under the impact of which others, more pessimistically inclined, might sink without a trace.

There were prisoners in German concentration camps during World War II whose positive outlook enabled them to rise above that tragedy to become great human beings—compassionate, forgiving, and wise.

Others, on the other hand, wallowing perennially in a sort of swamp of luxury, have been known to complain unceasingly of their lot in life merely because they were bored.

People's "specific gravity" makes them naturally, and in varying degrees, either positive or negative. To describe this variety in terms of a certain lightness or heaviness of consciousness is an apt metaphor, for it addresses the subjective awareness of every human being.

In every language, indeed, there are words that describe positive states of mind in terms of lightness—of rising or soaring awareness; and words also that describe negative states in terms of heaviness. We say, "I feel high," or "uplifted," or (to use a contemporary expression) "on cloud nine." And, again, we exclaim, "I feel low," or "downcast," or "in the dumps." It is unthinkable that anyone in his normal senses would say, "I feel wonderful!" when he feels spiritually heavy.

Everyone would like to rise from a feeling of inner heaviness toward lightness.

This metaphor, moreover, can be applied to over-all human development. For there are qualities—laziness, for example, and envy—that pull the mind downward. And there are others—kindness, and a spirit of willingness—that lift it upward.

Perhaps, if we study the qualities of personality in this context, we shall be able to discern a sort of universal progression that will serve teachers in their efforts to guide their students.

The important consideration will be to see whether the specific gravity, and not merely the fleeting moods, of a child can be changed. Certainly, it is with this deeper side of his nature that the teacher should be concerned.

Let us consider some of the contrasting qualities mentioned in the last chapter. To refresh memory, here they are again: expansive vs. contractive; outgoing vs. withdrawn; positive vs. negative; constructive vs. destructive; imaginative vs. literal; creative vs. imitative; aggressive vs. passive; assertive vs. submissive.

The first pair—expansive vs. contractive—instantly provides a clue. For it suggests the relative densities of matter. And the denser its matter, as we all know, the deeper an object will sink in water. The less dense, on the contrary, the higher it will rise, even up into the atmosphere.

An expansive nature, similarly, has much less specific spiritual gravity, whereas a contractive nature, with its tendency to relate everything back to itself, may be said to compact its energies.

A physicist might scoff at this correlation between psychological "density" and the relative density of matter. But the metaphor holds under examination. For a contractive, "compacted" nature *is* heavier, in the sense we've proposed. And an expansive, generous spirit *is,* in this sense, lighter.

Imagine consciousness as consisting of countless tiny particles. I don't suppose it is, really. But on the other hand, even light has been shown to be both a particle and a wave. So, for the purposes of metaphor—why not?

When these particles become compacted, as we might say they do in the case of the egotist, the focus of his attention being wholly inward upon himself, they assume a condition of greater density. But when they expand outward to include others in their field of awareness, their density becomes less. They rise, in consequence, toward a lighter, more joyful consciousness, even as a balloon filled with helium will rise in the air.

The more one's sympathies expand outward from self to include family and friends, neighbors, country, all mankind, and all creatures, the more the "particles" of his consciousness will spread outward—rendering him, in the process, increasingly "light," and inwardly free.

Selfish people are contractive, and therefore "heavy." Unselfish people are expansive, and therefore "light." Selfish people, moreover, in their mental heaviness, are forever unhappy, negative, even morose. But unselfish people, in their mental lightness, are always positive and cheerful.

Diverse psychological traits are united in the single phenomenon of relative "specific gravity," or psychological "density." Expansiveness, happiness, and a positive outlook share the quality of lightness. Contractiveness, unhappiness, and negativity, on the other hand, share a heaviness of spirit.

Take another of the contrasts above: that between an outgoing nature, and one that is withdrawn. Superficially—and so might they be judged in any popularity contest—it may seem that an outgoing nature is expansive, and a withdrawn nature, contractive. But on examining these two in the context of the "specific gravity" of each, we see that appearances can be deceiving.

For an outgoing nature may be merely egotistical and self-centered—and therefore, in the present context, dense. A withdrawn nature, on the other hand, may be contemplative; not self-preoccupied at all, but, in its inner expansiveness, enjoying a light specific gravity.

It is from within, and not superficially, that the individual child must be understood.

But would an outgoing, but ego-centered, nature, even if not expansive and light, fit into the same category of "heaviness" as, let us say, a nature that was dull-minded and slothful? Surely not. Obviously, there are gradations of density. "Heavy" and "light" are designations too black and white to cover in-between shadings of grey.

A third designation is needed, between "heavy" and "light." For clarity's sake, however, it should be better defined than, simply, "medium heavy," or, "medium light."

There is only one thing, really, that lifts one out of the depths, the spiritual "density" of dullness, laziness, and despair: intense activity of some kind. Visualization, meditation, counseling, positive thinking—none of these excessively "light" activities can come even close to doing the trick.

Action is the answer. And because we've described spiritual "density" as an intense focus of energy inward upon the ego, the way to lighten this density will be through activity that expands the ego by first affirming it, not denying it.

An outgoing but ego-affirming attitude, while admittedly detrimental to the attainment of sanctity, is the best possible cure for the negative egoism of a contractive spirit.

Let us, then, define this middle category as *"ego-active."*

A "light" nature may be active, too. In its expansiveness, however, there will be little density—that is to say, little focus of energy—at its egoic center. When such a person acts, he has a clear perception of the things he must do, and focuses on them with a minimum of ego-induced strain.

The "ego-active" nature, on the other hand, though more expanded than the "heavy" nature, is still strongly focused on its own center. In activity, such a person lacks the simplicity of clear purpose, and tends in his restlessness to kick up unnecessary clouds of mental dust, thereby obscuring anything that he hopes to clarify. His activity, like his consciousness, is never harmonious.

Consider, now, out of the above-mentioned qualities, these two: *constructive* vs. *destructive.* Where would these fit in the gradation of relative "density," or "specific spiritual gravity"? They are not necessarily *polar* opposites. The designation, *constructive,* might be applied equally well to both "ego-active" and "light" natures; the former particularly if it entailed building for ego-gratification, or without any useful purpose.

Destructive, on the other hand, might be applied to either "ego-active" or "heavy" personalities, depending on whether their tendency is only to destroy, or, more laudably, to destroy obstructions to egoic self-expression.

We see that it is possible to gauge a child's specific spiritual gravity—less so in terms of a vast array of psychological traits, and more so in vastly simplified terms of his "specific spiritual gravity," or "density," of consciousness.

Essentially, this relative density must be gauged by inner feeling—by intuition, if you will. It is doubtful whether the process could be reduced to an objective science. It depends too much on the perceptiveness of the individual teacher.

There *are,* however, objective criteria also.

Heaviness or lightness in a child's consciousness will be revealed, for one thing, in the attitudes of his body. A child whose outlook on life is "heavy" will actually look as if he felt heavy, inwardly: in his posture, in the slump of his shoulders, in his downward gaze. He will even walk or sit as if his weight were a burden to him.

A child of light consciousness, by contrast, will reveal by every gesture an inner feeling of lightness. He may raise his arms frequently, and not let them hang heavily at his sides. He will square his shoulders, instead of letting them sag. He will sit upright, gaze upward often, and walk energetically rather than lurch.

Again, a child's psychological "density" can be recognized in his choice of friends. Low energy children will shun, and may well resent, the company of those of high energy. The high energy child, on the other hand, will find little to interest him in those of low energy, and will tend to look for companionship to others of as high an energy level as his own.

But again, children may "mix downward" for special motives. If they do, the chances are that they won't do so more than one step below their own natural level. The child of middle, or "ego-active," energy may feel a call to help the spiritually "heavy" ones. And the child of high energy may, for similar motives, mix with those of "ego-active" energy.

The question here will be, What do their *motives* seem to be? Do they *identify* with their apparently "heavier" companions? Or are they only trying to help them?

Teachers may devise tests of a child's reactions to challenges. For instance, how readily does he share with others? How truthful is he? Does he respond positively to discipline? When asked to do something, does he habitually seek excuses? or does he respond willingly? Does he reveal a sense of responsibility? And does he show initiative?

Observe him at play. Is he basically cheerful when relaxed, or habitually glum? Does he set himself against others, or does he work with them? On the other hand—another alternative—does he set himself apart from them; and, if so, does he seem to do so in a self-enclosing way, or is it merely that the focus of his attention is elsewhere?

One might easily write a book on the various outward ways to gauge a child's natural "specific gravity." This is not the place, however, for such a dissertation. Suffice it here to repeat that the teacher's perception must be, above all, from within. Indeed, too much attention to outward details might only serve to obstruct subtler insight.

How, then, having once discovered the child's psychological, or spiritual, level, is the teacher to proceed toward helping him?

Obviously, a child's problems may reflect something external in his life—parents in the process of separating, for example, or a father with a drinking problem. Such possibilities must be considered first, and explored through sensitive questioning. But if, as happens more normally than most people realize, a low "specific gravity" is due specifically to the child's own nature, then it will be necessary for the teacher to do his best to raise the student's level of energy and consciousness.

Moreover, it needn't be a matter of addressing only the child with a problem. At every level of awareness, the direction of development should be upward. The well-adjusted child, too, can be shown how to become ever better adjusted and happier.

We have here, then, *three* psychological tools. The first is the child's "specific spiritual gravity," or normal level of awareness: from "heavy," through "ego-active," and upwards toward "light." Gradations in between will suggest themselves naturally, as well as the question of whether the general pull of various psychological traits is upward, or downward, and whether therefore these traits are to be encouraged, discouraged, or transmuted.

The second psychological tool is the actual means of accomplishing the child's transformation: not only upward, as with physical posture, dance movements, etc., but by working on what we have termed the degree of "density" of his consciousness. In the present context it would be confusing to speak, as one normally does, of "high" and "low" density, so let us use the terms, rather, *expansion* and *contraction*.

The direction of guidance should ever be toward expanding the child's sense of self-identity, his awareness. Care, on the other hand, should be taken not to force such expansion on him, but to let him blossom outward from within, of his own free will.

The third tool is motivation. How can the teacher get children to *want* to change their level of awareness and to expand their self-identity? By helping them to understand that by so doing they will escape pain and find happiness—or, if happy already, that they will increase their measure of happiness.

How are these tools to be used? Consciously, on the part of the teachers. But often, on the child's part, without his active awareness, lest by his self-consciousness everything be spoiled.

A specific tool not mentioned earlier is deep breathing. Such breathing is remarkably effective in drawing the energy from the lower to the upper parts of the body, and thus in creating a literal sense of soaring, upward movement.

Wholesome exercise is invigorating, and will help the child to direct a flow of energy outwardly that might otherwise be too easily focused inward upon himself.

A school which I attended for two years in England as a boy had an ingenious system for inspiring children to greater individual effort. It graded us not only in our studies, but also with colors, for how hard we'd tried. "Excellent" was a double red oblong on our grading papers. "Very good" was a single red oblong; "good," a double green; "fair," a single green. "Poor" was a double blue; and "very poor," a single blue. Somehow, we tended to work much harder for those colors than we ever did for merely numerical grades.

Try, if possible, to help the child in his selection of companions. Choose those with qualities that will help to expand his sympathies and uplift his consciousness.

And remember, finally, the importance to the child of *your* magnetism. Live as much as possible, yourself, on a high level of awareness. The more expanded *you* are, the more expanded he is likely to become.

12

Every Child an Einstein?

I REMEMBER, as a child, practicing the piano assiduously for hours at a time. I loved it, though I can't say I came within even hailing distance of the child prodigies around. My mother, however,—bless all mothers!—used to tell me, "If you want to, there's no reason you can't become a concert pianist."

What mother wouldn't like to believe that her little Jimmy might someday become President, or a Michelangelo, a famous scientist, or a great saint?

But—well, let's face it: How likely is it?

Every teacher worthy of the name, too, would like to be able to inspire his students to rise to the heights of success and fame.

But, again—let's face it: How likely is it?

The problem isn't only that there are so few great spirits born in any age. Much worse: our educational system actively *discourages* greatness.

To begin with, the premise of the system is that the dullest student is entitled to the same education as the brightest. No one, of course, would want to deny it to him. The problem lies in the way we've gone at it—that is, in the fact that we've directed the major focus of our attention toward the lowest level.

It takes little to inspire a child of "light specific gravity" to soar. Considerably greater effort is needed to get an "ego-active" child to inch his way upward. And for anyone whose "specific gravity" is really heavy, it may take a massive effort to budge him at all.

One must, of course, do one's best, even for the dullest. Indeed, with dull students, too, one may sometimes succeed remarkably. For human beings are a mixture of many traits. A child with the heaviest consciousness may possess some vital, self-expanding trait, by which, if emphasized, he might be helped to rise far above anyone's expectations of him.

But is this the success we want to point to as justification for our educational system? Is it to be our sole boast that we've made our dullest students into useful members of society? It would be desirable also, surely, to be able to point to the geniuses we've produced—especially if, in the process, we hadn't penalized the dull.

It isn't even fair to the bright students to give them so little attention. With so much energy directed toward those at the bottom of the ladder, excellence becomes, in a sense, punished. And not even mediocrity gets much of a chance.

The bright student suffers. But so also does society. For the world *needs* great men and women, both for what they accomplish in themselves, and for what they inspire in others.

Schools should be places where the best is brought out in children. Instead, owing largely to an emphasis on merely discouraging the worst in them, this is in fact what we often get: the worst. One achieves what one concentrates on.

It isn't ever easy to admit to oneself that dull children really *are* dull. Moreover, it is only charitable to give them every chance to receive the same education that the brightest receive. But problems arise when, instead of merely offering them this chance, one tries to force that same education down their throats.

Facts cannot be dealt with so long as they are denied. And, let us face it, there are tendencies so deeply rooted in some children's natures that it may be best simply to accept them as they are. Only then may we be able to do something constructive to help them, without in the process cheating others.

For a child with a "heavy" nature, in terms of his "specific spiritual gravity," is likely to be dull-witted, slow, and more adept at using his body than his mind. How to inspire him to change? He probably isn't even interested in self-improvement. Try to expand his sympathies, and he'll very likely reply in terms of what others are, or are not, giving *him*.

Even one such child in the classroom can drag the overall level of teaching down into the abyss. If ignored, on the other hand, or even joked about by fellow students for his slow wit, he may gang up with others of similarly "heavy" consciousness to create trouble for everyone else in the school.

The "heavy-gravity" student may be inspired to ego-motivated action. Never, however, until firmly established on an ego-active level, will he rise, except in sporadic bursts, to action that is unselfishly motivated.

The best the teacher may accomplish with him is to teach him through a rudimentary system of punishment and reward: "Don't do that *if you know what's good for you*"; or, "Do that, and I'll buy you something good to eat." In this way, a few good habits may be inculcated in him that will stand him in good stead later in life, even if he isn't quite sure how or why they're right.

All this, however, is compromise. The basic problem remains: How to educate everyone without cheating anyone? Is it the answer to have separate classrooms—even separate schools? A grading system, *A* to *D,* for each separate classroom or school, with a sub-classification indicating in which one the student has studied?

All these are possible solutions. For present purposes, however, they seem remote and impracticable.

There is another, and better, solution. It is suggested by the old country school house, where one teacher was obliged to instruct all twelve grades. There was only one way that that system could be made to work: The teacher had to enlist the help of older students to instruct the younger.

The difference, in the present context, is that we are not thinking of one teacher for an entire school. It isn't a question, then, of older children teaching the younger. Rather, our concern is with students of the same age, but of diverse spiritual "densities."

My proposal concerns a shift of emphasis, of direction. At present, the view is *upward* from below, in the sense of bringing the low students up to a level where, it is hoped, all will be able to move onwards together.

Here is the proposal: Instead of, in this sense, working

upward from below, why not work *downward* from above?

How? Quite simply, by enlisting the help of "lighter" students to uplift the "heavier."

We have already seen that "ego-active" students may voluntarily mix with those of "heavy" consciousness, and that "light" students, similarly, may mix with "ego-active" students. The motive in both cases is usually not so much the gratification of friendly rapport as it is to help those below them.

"Heavy" students generally show little inclination, in any case, to listen to their teachers. But they will often listen to, and follow, children of their own age, who are more aware and magnetic than themselves. And whereas "ego-active" students may be more prone than the "heavy" students to heed their teachers, they, too, are inclined rather to follow their more magnetic peers.

If the "heavier" member of such an association is even slightly receptive, the magnetic exchange resulting from the company of another, more positive student may help to nudge him up the ladder toward a higher state of consciousness.

In the context of an "Education for Life," moreover, the student of relatively expansive awareness actually gains by helping others of more contractive awareness than himself. It is not as though, by teaching the slow learners, he were depriving himself of further study. The more he shares with others the living principles he has learned, the more he practices and strengthens his awareness of those principles in himself. In this way, no one loses. And everyone gains.

It is ironic that the very students who are the most inclined to learn from their teachers, and the most capable of doing so, are generally those who receive from them the least.

What every teacher ought to do, instead, is assiduously cultivate leadership qualities in any student who shows an inclination to reach down and help others below him.

There remains, of course, the danger of such students developing into "teachers' pets," and thus becoming universally despised by the other students. But there are ways around this pitfall.

First, and most obviously, teachers should be trained to be aware of the danger, and to make their selections on an impersonal basis, perhaps also with the help of other teachers. Because human nature is weak, however, it won't suffice merely to admonish teachers to avoid the pitfall of favoritism.

Rather, students selected to help others should form councils of their own. "Light," or expansive, students should be given one emphasis in their leadership, and "ego-active" students another. Obviously, sensitive issues are raised here which can only be worked out in living situations, since these change with every class.

The important thing is to realize that human magnetism is a fact of life. High-energy people are magnetic. And low-energy people lack magnetism, invariably.

What is meant by magnetism? Certainly, it doesn't mean that a compass will veer from true north and point to people of high energy! Still, magnetism is a fact of which everyone is, if only dimly, aware.

It might be compared to the magnetic field created by a

flow of electricity through a copper wire: the higher the voltage, the stronger the field. The higher the energy of a person, similarly, the greater his personal magnetism.

Much might be written on this subject. The important point here is for the teacher to realize that he will get nowhere at all if he encourages the merely "goody-goody" student to assume a leadership role. The child who is always prompt, willing, and supportive may seem at first the ideal choice. Unfortunately, such a child is often good merely because he wants ego-approval, or because he lacks the energy to kick up his heels.

Energy, then, must be included as a vital criterion. The child of low energy, but of eternally good will, is sure to lack the magnetism to attract and inspire others. Only in high-energy children can real leadership be developed.

And of course, high-energy students are among those the least likely to develop into teachers' pets.

Don't, therefore, seek out the "yes"-children to implement your programs. And don't be afraid at least to consider those of high-energy who are slow to follow. For these less malleable ones, once they've thought a proposal through, will often be among the most dedicated to any responsibility they accept.

Avoid, like the poison it is, an over-emphasis on personalities. Concentrate always, rather, on principles.

And don't be afraid to pose challenges. A great weakness exhibited by far too many teachers is the tendency, in their effort to get the children on their side, to play up to them. If you will look back over your own school years, I think you will see that the teachers who were the most universally admired, even loved, by the students were those who were scrupulously fair, who stuck by their principles, and who never succumbed to the temptation to do something merely because they thought they would be liked for it.

Children, themselves steeped in the ego-craving for acceptance by others, are highly sensitive to this weakness in others. They quickly discern, and despise, it in others, especially in their elders—and even more especially in their teachers, whom they look to for help in their climb up the steep mountain slopes to maturity.

13

The Case Against Atheism

IN QUEENSLAND, AUSTRALIA, a few years ago I was giving a seminar on some of the principles contained in this book. A man approached me afterwards.

"I entered the room toward the end of your talk," he said. "and heard you refer to God. Now then, I'm an atheist. How would you define God in such a way as to be meaningful to me?"

"Why not try thinking of Him," I suggested, "as the highest potential you can imagine for yourself?"

He stood there for a moment, surprised. Then he concluded, "Well, that's a definition I can live with!"

Mankind *needs* something to look up to—an ideal, a dream, an aspiration. We may think of that ideal as God, forever *consciously* awaiting and encouraging us to seek Him. Or we may think of it as merely some consciously held goal. In any case, the goal is, in a sense, conscious, for in our minds the attainment of it implies something to do with consciousness, a *conscious* fulfillment. Certainly, it is no wooden idol.

So then, for heaven's sake, why *not* call it God?

Voltaire said, "If God didn't exist, man would need to invent Him."

I'm not referring to a "God of the Christians," or a "God of the Jews." For that matter, among Christians, Jews, Hindus, and Moslems there are probably as many concepts of God as there are worshipers. The very word, *God,* is spoken merely by the human tongue. It is highly doubtful that this word—in English, no less!—reverberates through the universe.

Some people will imagine the Deity as Michelangelo's God, creating Adam on the ceiling of the Sistine Chapel. Others will imagine him as Krishna, smilingly playing the flute to attract souls away from ego-attachment. To still others, "He" will be a "She": a Universal Mother. Again, to some, God will be an impersonal Light, or Love, or Consciousness.

People have fought wars over their definitions of God, not realizing that even within their own ranks there was never unanimity. For whatever the words they used, the concept of each believer could only be born of his particular experience of life. The experiences of no two people on earth can be exactly alike.

I remember, when I was young, trying to visualize God as a Universal Mother. The thought of divine compassion as a feminine quality attracted me. I wasn't familiar with Roman Catholicism, with its many images of the Madonna. The best I could come up with, eventually, was a mental image of my godfather's wife, a sweet-tempered, motherly lady who had never been put in the uncomfortable position of having to discipline me.

Will somebody scold me as a blasphemer for holding such a concept? You see, I knew perfectly well that "Aunt Anna" wasn't God. It was just that thinking of her helped to conjure up in my mind the qualities of kindness and compassion on which I wanted to focus. In prayer, I passed eventually from this mental image to a sense of something more real—a higher, listening Presence.

The point is that even though no mental concept can ever fully define God, this doesn't mean that we ought therefore to abandon mental concepts altogether, and get on with the prosaic job of gathering in facts, facts, facts, like so many bundles of sheaves. (Odd, is it not? that professors, who so love every sort of intellectual theory, will generally avoid any mention of this particular mental concept, because, they say, it is "only" a theory!)

I'm not offering it as a theory, however, but as a universal human need. God is, if you like, but a word. But what this word stands for is the universal need to be inspired, to experience a higher reality than that of a filled belly, to be uplifted from the heavy mud of unknowing into the free sky of an expanded, ever lighter awareness. It is something we all need. Why, then, quibble about the word?

The problem is that the whole bias of modern thinking, and therefore of modern education, is—as we saw in the last chapter—toward the depths. Science came along a few centuries ago and said, "Look, we can't prove God, or heaven, or angels. But we *can* prove mass, weight, and motion. So let's stick with these." Some of those scientists were, in fact, devout believers. They were trying to evolve a new approach to reality, however, based on provable facts.

It was an excellent idea. Moreover, it is amazing how vast and complex is the universe that science has revealed to us after only four hundred years of this apparently simplistic approach to reality—a universe of hundreds of billions of stars and galaxies; a picture of things that would have been dismissed as the ravings of a lunatic had it been suggested even a century ago!

In leaving God out of scientific reckoning, however, the impression left, now that science has won the day for its method, is that God should be left out of *all* rational reckoning, even when dealing with human issues, issues of morals and values, and not with the measurable fundamentals of physics and chemistry.

In the last century, Darwin claimed that mankind is descended, in a manner of speaking, from the monkeys. People were already schooled by his day to think of matter, and not man, as the proper concern of man. Now, with Darwin's help, man came to be seen as the product of material atoms gradually coalescing, then evolving by accidental selection, to produce what we are pleased to consider the civilized creature that he is today.

Freud, following this natural ideational progression, explained human nature in terms of a basic sex drive, and of various related abnormalities. Other psychologists later explained man in terms of other simplifications—Adler, for example, with his equally Darwinian emphasis on a desire for power (a product, one supposes, of the struggle for survival).

In these views, man *is* his lower nature, and merely glosses over the fact when he pretends to have ideals. In these views, then, if you know anyone who believes deeply in divine love, you'd do well to guard your daughters.

Well, for that matter, why bother? If our only reality is

this lower nature of ours, why not, with Sartre, and in the modern vernacular, "Go for it"?

Modern education, consciously or unconsciously, is founded on this bottom-upward view of things. And the churches have made the worst possible case for their own higher view, both by losing their tempers and hurling perpetual anathemas, and by insisting on substituting definitions—that is to say, dogmas—for reality. They've given the educators the best imaginable excuse for *not* including God in the classroom. For religionists on all sides are heard shouting at one another: "God is *this!*" "No, no, you fool, He is *that!*"

Scientists, at least, agree that the sun and moon are more or less what they've observed them to be. With so much disagreement in the churches, then, why *should* the schools deal with a subject that is, evidently, unteachable?

And yet, our children long for something more than dry facts. They long to be told that there is indeed something worthwhile to believe in, to hope for. Yes, they long for ideals.

Knock out the concept of God, and you knock out the very basis of civilization.

We have already seen that moral and spiritual values need not be confined to the many sectarian teachings regarding them. Humility, for example, is quite unnecessarily called *Christian* humility; it is humility, simply, and only limited by the additional label, "Christian."

Why can't we do the same thing with the concept of God? Why buy the various labels that have been stuck onto Him by those in religion who claim to speak in His name?

Why speak of a "Christian" God, or a "Jewish" God?

Why not consider the possibility that there might even be an "atheists' " God?

For though the atheist claims to reject God altogether, all he really rejects is other people's definitions. For himself, he *must* be motivated by some ideal, some goal, some principle, or else abandon his very humanity. And that principle, for him, is what we call God, for it is the highest point toward which he himself presently aspires.

Granted, his may not be another person's high principle. Yet I venture to say that there is *no* principle that the limited human mind can conceptualize that can hold up its head and say with absolute conviction, "I, finally, *am* God!"

In 1960, I attended an interfaith conference in India. It had been organized by a young, idealistic Jain monk who wanted to get representatives of the major world religions to agree on a set of tenets that would enable them to present a united front against the threat of materialism.

The delegates used the conference, instead, as a platform for those aspects of their beliefs which separated them one from another.

As they spoke, I found myself imagining them trying actually to agree on some universal tenet. Clearly, it wouldn't be easy.

Someone might propose, as self-evident for the followers of any religion, a belief in God. But to this proposal the Buddhists would object: No, they couldn't subscribe to such a statement. Buddhism is atheistical.

Well, then, what about getting everyone to agree that there is life after death? Here, too, certain religions would have to abstain.

In the nineteen fifties, someone made a study of the major world religions, and found one point only on which all agreed: Every religion, he pointed out, teaches some variant of the saying, "Whatsoever you want others to do unto you, do that unto them." It was an interesting study. But it left me with the thought, "And for this end we need *religion?*"

It seems little more than the sort of solution that any civilized human being would hit upon, merely by living in the society of others. A philosophy, in other words, of enlightened self-service. Any person of common sense might have said the same. It would have been strange, indeed, if the great religions had *not* added some such statement to their teachings.

No, what all the great religions really do is endeavor to inspire man in some way to raise his consciousness, to make it less "dense" in the sense given the word in this book, less ego-centered, and more expansive. This is not, perhaps, a *stated* tenet of all of them, but it is certainly a universal effect.

Even Shintoism, a ceremonial religion which more or less limits itself to marrying and burying its adherents, offers them in the process a sense of the harmony and fitness of things. As such, it fosters in them a *consciousness* of harmony—one aspect, surely, of an uplifted awareness.

It is time, and long past time, that we reinstituted the reality of high values and ideals. Indeed, is it not self-evident that man is not only pushed upward from below, but also *drawn* upward, from above? If even science speaks of potential energy as actual energy, why dismiss human potentials as unreal? The very fact that they are there *as potentials* makes them real enough for any scientific discussion (if science must remain the criterion).

Man is not diverted from reality by his dreams, his fantasies, his ideals. Far truer would it be to admit that a great deal of reality is revealed to him by them. For once stomachs have been filled, bodies clothed, and man's living space protected from the elements, there remains a basic hunger which no amount of possessions, power, pleasure, or protection can fulfill: the hunger to know, to understand, to participate with wonder in ever broader vistas of universal reality.

Children cannot be forced to learn. And mankind cannot be merely pushed up the ladder toward final awakening. One must be attracted upward, by the response of his free will.

That magnet, finally, which has ever drawn him upward is what we know—dimly, but, let us hope, with growing comprehension—as God.

14

The Tools of Maturity

AN ASTRONOMER, bent on scanning the heavens, needs an accurately ground telescope, and one that is free of dust. A carpenter, building a house, needs tools that are well made and well maintained. A jeweller, dealing in precious stones that he weighs in fractions of a carat, needs a highly sensitive scale; a simple bathroom scale would be hopelessly inadequate for his work.

In every department of life, tools are needed. In the modern age, especially, great care is devoted to their development and maintenance.

It is surprising, in this context, how little attention is paid to the "ultimate tool"—that on which every human being must rely: his own self—his body and brain.

The physical body, if not treated with sensitive respect, will end up becoming one's worst enemy, obstructing every effort of the will to advance toward any goal. And the brain that is clouded, unfocused, or overwhelmed by emotional storms will perceive nothing clearly, no matter how excellent the material instruments one uses.

Our modern school system concentrates on imparting outward information, but devotes almost no attention to developing the student's ability to *absorb* this information. It gives him outward tools, but never even suggests to him methods for developing his powers of concentration, his memory, his ability to think clearly.

In one of my classes when I was in school, if any student seemed unable to grasp a point under discussion, the teacher would inquire with jocular solicitude, "What's the matter, Jones?" (if that was his name) "Are you in love?" Strange to say, this was the only recognition the student ever received of the possible importance of his emotions to the total learning process.

Even in such basic matters as diet, how much are our children taught? They are given what has come to be called "junk" food (for one example), high in sugar content. Does no one ever tell them that too much sugar clouds the ability to think clearly?

In matters of physical exercise, they are involved in violent sports that will stand them in no useful stead later in life, and that may even permanently injure their bodies. But how much attention is paid to teaching them forms of exercise that will benefit them throughout their lives?

Exercise should be approached in the manner of a long distance runner, with clear recognition given to the fact that the physical body may have to serve its owner for another seventy or eighty years, and ought not to be treated as though whatever exercise it gets will end at high school or college graduation.

A young friend of mine, an excellent skier, several years ago was in the habit of making jumps that, because of her skill, she survived joyfully, but that jarred every bone in her body. Wisely, she abandoned the practice when her physician told her, "If you go on like this, by the time you're forty-five you'll be confined to a wheel chair."

Children would soon, of course, become bored if all the exercise they were permitted were a daily trudge around the compound. Certainly, I'm not referring to tiresome exercise! Even walking and hiking, however, can be delightful when pursued in the broad, open countryside, breathing in fresh air, and feasting one's gaze on beautiful hills and green fields.

The will power, moreover, needs challenges too if it is to be properly developed. In this sense at least, strenuous sports very definitely serve a useful purpose in education.

But I *am* pleading for the addition of common sense, for a view to life's longer rhythms, and for physical development and the sorts of exercise that will stand the child in good stead throughout his life.

The other day, for example, my brain was feeling foggy, and no amount of flogging it with affirmations of energy could get it to stagger out into the sunlight of clear thought. I then left my desk and jogged for ten minutes on a trampoline. The subsequent difference in my mental clarity was amazing.

A steady routine of exercise is important for everyone— one that doesn't require a football field and two teams to bludgeon one another into semi-paralysis, but one that is pleasant, and even fun, to follow. This habit should be inculcated in children, even in those with a greater fondness for intellectual pursuits.

Good diet, right exercise, regular exposure to sunlight and fresh air: These can develop the body as a tool for the long-range efficiency of the entire being.

* * *

And then there is the question of the emotions. How many adults—what to speak of children?—recognize the difference between emotion and feeling? Very few.

And how many children, consequently, are taught that calm, sensitive feeling is an invaluable tool for complete understanding? Or that *turbulent* feelings—which is to say, emotions—can prevent clear understanding on any level?

Again, very few.

Few children, again, are taught the extent to which reason is *influenced* by feeling, but *distorted* by the emotions. And few are taught that by developing calm feeling they will improve their understanding of objective reality.

Feeling, when calm and refined, is important to mature insight. And there are ways of clarifying feeling, just as there are ways, commonly taught in school as the principles of logic, by which one can learn to reason correctly. The ways of clarifying feeling include, for instance, learning how to remove feeling from personal likes and dislikes, in order to arrive at what, at one's calm inner center, one *really perceives* about any given situation.

Only by this kind of calm inner certainty can one recognize the right course to take in any action. And those who guide their lives from this deeper level of feeling achieve levels of success that are never reached by people who expect by thinking alone to get their answers. Reason, on the other hand, unaided by feeling, can point in hundreds of equally plausible directions, and leave one with no certainty as to the rightness of any of them.

Children need to learn how to react *appropriately*, and not merely from a level of emotional subjectivity. Considerable training is necessary for them to learn how to harness their feelings, and to make of them a useful ally. Nothing, virtually, of this kind of training is given in the schools.

What they *are* taught, instead, is that feelings in general obstruct true perception. They are given the scientific method as a model. "If you want to see things realistically," they are told, "you must be objective. This means you must always separate reason from feeling, and view life in cold terms of logic."

Ignored is the fact that, usually, the greater the scientist, the more deeply he *feels* his commitment to his field. Or that, as Einstein put it, the essence of true scientific discovery is a sense of mystical wonder.

Feeling can never, in any case, be suppressed in human nature. Shove it under water at this point over here— where at least you can see and perhaps deal with it—and it will only pop up over there, where you least expect it. And many times, when it has in fact leapt out at people unrecognized, it has incited to riot.

Feeling, then, is a vital tool for achieving true maturity. It must be recognized and encouraged in the right way, and not simply ignored, suppressed, or treated as something about which nothing reasonable can be done.

* * *

There is a third tool of maturity: the *will power.*
I am not familiar with the exact statistics, but in any

given year hundreds of businesses are started, yet only a few ever succeed. Read any success story. The one thing that stands out in all of them is the *will power* expressed in the life of every person who ever made it to the top.

Successful people can't even imagine saying, "I can't." If they find that one method doesn't work, they'll try another, and another, and keep on trying until they find one that does work.

How often we find people losing courage after one or two half-hearted attempts at doing something! And how often do we find them imagining that a job is already finished, merely because they've talked about it, or outlined it on paper! How often, again, do we find people giving up after encountering a mere smattering of obstacles, excusing themselves with the words, "It wasn't meant to be." (That favorite excuse of cowards!)

Business colleges fill their students' brains with marketing techniques, organizational charts, and secrets of profitable investment. They send graduates out into the world with the impression that all this knowledge will be their guarantee of success. How is it, graduates later wonder, that so few ever made the grade?

Even more incomprehensible to them is the large number of highly successful business people whose theoretical training is far less than their own. How did that steel tycoon earn his millions, for example? Good heavens, he never even finished high school!

The answer is perfectly simple: He stuck to it.

No one can really succeed in life without will power. The will, then, is a vital ingredient of maturity, and should be emphasized as such in the schools. Techniques should bc taught for developing it, and opportunities explored for expressing it.

* * *

The fourth and final tool of maturity is the intellect. One may say, "Here at least is one faculty to which we need pay no special attention. Modern education is already fully devoted to its development."

Devoted, perhaps, but not to its full development. For when the intellect is treated as a thing apart from the other three tools of maturity—body, feeling, and will power—it grows like a sort of poorly nourished and anemic plant: tall, perhaps, but colorless and fragile.

One weakness of the intellect is, as we have seen, its tendency to soar up, up and away like a balloon into clouds of fascinating theory, while carelessly discarding the weighty ballast of fact. A balanced awareness of physical realities, as experienced first of all *through the body,* is necessary, if man is to develop his intellect as a useful faculty.

Another weakness of the intellect is, as we have seen also, its tendency to substitute theory for action—even to consider itself betrayed by cloddish reminders of the need for action. Regular, daily doses of will power are necessary to prevent this weakness from degenerating into mental paralysis.

A third weakness is—and here *feeling* becomes involved—the temptation of intellectuality to imagine itself so clever that it can actually *create* truth. There comes upon certain people of exceptional intelligence a sort of Olympian delusion: the thought that, by reason alone,

107

they can demonstrate conclusively anything they desire. Is it their wish to prove that black is white, or white, black? No problem! They imagine themselves capable of reasoning truth into, or out of, existence, purely according to whatever they want it to be.

We see here, indeed, the danger of suppressing feeling: It will rise again, and again and again, as Michael Ende said in *The Never-Ending Story,* in the form of the most fantastic lies.

Reason is rightly guided only when it acknowledges the inescapability of cosmic law—that is to say, of what *is.*

Thus, the intellect must be developed in constant reference to demonstrable truths. Webs of logic finely spun from nothing more substantial than an intriguing fancy, or a quotation, must be referred again and again to reality to see how true they are.

A further point is that the intellect needs to be developed along *useful* lines. Of what value, for example, a wonderful plan for battle, entailing the deployment of ten thousand troops, when all one has in fact are a hundred foot-weary soldiers?

And what is the use of exclaiming proudly, "The operation was a success!"—when, in fact, the patient died peacefully on the operating table?

The intellect, finally, must be developed in full recognition that it is a tool, merely, wielded by the hand, but never itself wielding the hand. It can be used rightly or wrongly, depending on one's respect for other, higher, and immutable realities.

A human being, in order to function fully and effectively in this world, needs to develop in himself these four tools of maturity: physical energy and control; emotional calmness and expansiveness; dynamic, persistent will power; and a clear, practical intellect.

Remove any one of these aspects from the others, and it becomes weakened and distorted. Each depends for its perfection on the other three.

A person of great physical energy and control, but with undeveloped feelings, will power, or intelligence, will be little more than an animal, responding to every stimulus on a purely instinctual level.

A person of sensitively refined feelings, but underdeveloped in the other three aspects of maturity, will too easily lose himself in hypochondria or in other nameless fears.

A person, on the other hand, of strong will power, but deficient in the other three tools of maturity, may compensate for his physical weakness by developing a tyrannical nature. Lack of emotional control may plunge him into violent rages against anyone so presumptuous as to oppose him on the smallest issue. And an undeveloped intellect may lead him to commit actions that are unbridled, because never viewed in the light of introspection.

We have seen, finally, the deficiency of the intellect when unsupported by the other three "tools," as I have called them, of maturity.

An interesting point is that these tools are best developed in sequence: body first, then feeling, next will power, and last of all, the intellect.

Feeling, for example, needs grounding in a firm sense of physical reality if it is really to inspire and uplift, instead of running maudlin. Will power, when developed without reference both to physical energy and to physically balanced emotions, can lead to ruthlessness, or to purposeless explosions of energy.

In the child's development, therefore, care should be given not only to teaching him the right use of his body, feelings, will power, and intellect, but also to leading him through these, in the proper sequence, to maturity.

15

The Stages of Maturity

CERTAIN MEDICINES are designed to release their healing properties into the body gradually, at periods of a few hours each.

Certain changes in the human body, similarly, are programed to occur at definite stages of a person's life.

At about six years, the child begins to lose his baby teeth and to grow new ones suitable to an adult body. At twelve, roughly, he undergoes the physical, mental, and emotional changes that come with puberty. At about eighteen, his body stops growing. Women, more or less at forty-eight, enter menopause with its attendant mental and emotional trials.

The changes people undergo in life are not only the result of physical alterations. There is, for example, the well-known "mid-life crisis." And there is the psychological need, around age 60, to withdraw from intense outward involvements.

It has even been found statistically that certain mental abilities reach their peak strength at certain ages: mathematics and poetry, for example, in a person's late teens to early twenties; business acumen, in his fifties; philosophical insight, in his sixties and seventies.

The stages of life make a fascinating study. Various

explanations have been offered for them. Astrologers, for example, relate the most significant of them to the cycles of Jupiter and Saturn: Jupiter, for the development of man's inner life; Saturn, for the cycles governing his outer world, including his life's work.

It may be only coincidence, but the twelve-year cycles of Jupiter—six years of movement away from the point of origin in the birth chart, and six years of inward return—do correspond to certain developments in the life of man. If nothing else, then, they at least make a useful peg on which to hang our recognition of these developments.

Observable, for example, in the child's psychological and spiritual development are four specific, progressive, stages. At each of these he finds it natural to assume responsibility for developing one of the basic "tools," as I've described them, of maturity.

The first six years of life are taken up primarily with the development of physical awareness. The next six—until roughly the age of twelve—are the best years for learning emotional refinement and control. From twelve to eighteen, teenage rebelliousness points clearly to a natural focus on the development of will power. And the last six years, from eighteen to twenty-four, are the natural time of life for developing the intellect.

These four phases of development can easily be paired off to make two cycles of twelve years each: physical/emotional, and will power/intellect. The first of each pair—bodily awareness, and the development of will power—suggests a more outward direction of the ego. The second of each—emotional refinement, and intellectual awakening—seems to suggest a more inward direction.

There is indeed, then, a correlation between these two twelve-year stages of human development and the twelve-year cycles of Jupiter, with their six years of outward projection and six of inward return.

But again, we may point also to a correlation between these four stages of maturity and fundamental changes that take place in the physical body: the appearance, at about six years of age, of the child's first permanent teeth; the advent of puberty at about the age of twelve; and the cessation of physical development at about eighteen.

These may be only convenient memory pegs. But the four stages of maturity, with pegs or without, are readily observable facts.

Friends of mine, for example, who teach children the Suzuki method for playing the violin, have informed me that, until the age of six, their students are fully occupied with the sheer physical mechanics of playing. From six to twelve years, they are moved by the beauty of the music. And from twelve onwards, through high school, they labor determinedly at mastering technique.

The first thing a baby needs to learn is how to handle his body. At first, he can only wave his arms and legs in the air helplessly. Then, he begins to crawl, then toddle, and finally to run. Even as late as his sixth year, the child is still physically awkward, colliding with things as he runs, dropping bottles as he removes their caps, scattering food with his fork as he feeds himself.

Beyond muscular control, the child's first six years are a time of sensory awakening to the world around him. Sights, sounds, smells, tastes, the tantalizing feel of things to the touch—all these have, for him, an amazingly vivid reality. The rainbow colors of the sunlight in a dewdrop; the distinctive tread of each member of his household; fragrant morning smells in the kitchen; the smooth feeling of clean sheets—these impressions and many others flood his consciousness.

Through his body, then, and through his developing sensory awareness, he can be taught most easily.

At about the age of six, he is ready to develop emotionally. This doesn't mean that he hasn't been emotionally aware until then. Far from it! During those first six years of life his subjective awareness may have attained to no other level. But at six begins his time for refining his emotions.

It is, above all, from this time onward that the child can be inspired to noble sentiments. These six years are a time of hero worship. They are a time, therefore, to offer him constructive role models—in legend, in fantasy, in history, and in present reality.

At twelve years, or thereabouts, with the onset of puberty, the ego begins to assert itself more aggressively. With this assertion comes an awakened need to test and strengthen the will power. The important thing now will be to guide the adolescent toward the right, expansive use of his will power. He must learn self-control, rather than trying to dominate others, or to prove himself in their eyes.

Bodily awareness at this time will assume new meaning for him, and must be channeled healthfully, through sports and other vigorous exercise. He must learn, also, how to channel his physical energies creatively, toward constructive activities of various kinds, depending on his own nature.

This is a time in the developing child's life when his encrgics can with equal ease sink or rise in the scale of heaviness and lightness. Without proper guidance and stimulation, he may become contractive, dwelling on himself only, and his own problems (if he is introverted); or entering into intense ego competition with others (if his nature is outgoing). Properly guided, however, this can become a wonderful period of active idealism.

It is a mistake to write off the teen-age years as merely a period to be, if possible, survived. I even wonder whether much of the problem that children face in their teens is not due to the powerfully negative image projected onto them at this time of their lives by adults.

It is painfully evident, to parents especially, that adolescents are no longer the sweet, innocent, trustful,—dare I say it?—cuddly children of yesterday. Infants, and the very young of all species, have something beautiful that—in a sense to everyone's regret—they lose as they grow up. It isn't merely their small size. A baby elephant, after all, is already larger than an adult human being. Rather, it is the trust we see in their eyes. They haven't yet learned to suspect the intentions of an indifferent or hostile world.

Jim Corbett, the famous tiger hunter, did what he called his favorite hunting with a camera. One day he was lying in a tree on a machan, his camera ready, when he saw a grown Bengal tiger stalking a kid goat. At some point in the tiger's advance the kid heard him, and turned around. Beholding this strange, enormous creature, it tottered over and began to sniff at him curiously.

Well, what could the tiger do? It rose up, and, to save face, allowed itself to be sniffed at a while longer. Then with great dignity it turned and strode off into the jungle.

115

The infant's sweet innocence is lost, not only in mankind, but in all animals, with the advent of sexual maturity. Parents, especially mothers, cannot fail to feel the loss. (I'll never forget my own mother's response when I, at the age of forty-five, gave her a birthday card showing a big bruiser of a man with stubble chin, chewing a cigar out of the side of his mouth, but dressed in a little sailor suit with short pants, and holding a balloon. The message read, "Happy birthday, Mommy, from your little boy." How my mother laughed!)

Nevertheless, adolescence is an inevitable change. It must therefore be made a *good* change. And this it can become, partly, by projecting positive expectations onto the growing child.

Proper training during the first twelve years, and proper reference, afterwards, to the values learned during those years, will be a great aid in turning this third six-year stage into a time of real opportunity.

At eighteen, the child is ready to develop his intellect. Much more than learning to reason cleverly—a skill that he may indeed have shown already by the age of three!—this is a period for learning to reason *clearly,* from a sense of discernment and discrimination.

At twenty-four there is, perhaps, no obvious biological change, such as one finds at the beginning of each of the other stages, to suggest that after six years of intellectual unfoldment the child is ready to enter the world of adulthood. In fact, college usually lasts only four years, after which one is expected to get out there and shoulder adult responsibilities with everyone else. From my own observation of young people at that age, however, I am inclined to recommend that they not be forced out of the learning mode until they turn twenty-four.

From the beginning of life, children are often found more inclined by nature to feel, to will, or to reason. An intellectually gifted child, for example, may reveal this gift almost with the first words he utters. And an infant with a naturally strong will power will probably make this power felt in the cradle. There have, however, been many brilliant people, even geniuses, who were unbalanced, and therefore unsuccessful, as human beings. And there have been many men of great will power who were yet lacking in human feeling.

Whatever the child's intrinsic ability, then, it would be wise not to cheat him of his natural development, through the four stages of maturity. While giving recognition to his intellectual needs, for example, remember also that a six-year-old is still a child, and that the other aspects of his human nature must be brought to maturity also, if he is eventually to live a full, and fulfilled, life.

16

The Foundation Years

THE FIRST SIX, OR PRE-SCHOOL, YEARS of a child's life
are the most important for establishing habits that will last
him a lifetime. Great care should be taken to inculcate in him
wholesome habits, tastes, and attitudes. It is at this age, especially, that the adage holds: "As the twig inclineth, so doth
the tree grow."

For this reason also it would be good for the child to be en-
rolled in a pre-school of some kind, to learn with others, and
under a teacher who is trained in methods of instruction of
which few parents have any direct experience.

During his first six years, as we have seen, a child can learn
best through the medium of his body, and by developing his
awareness through his five senses.

Muscular and motor control is, perhaps, the most difficult
lesson in the beginning. The small child needs to be made
progressively aware of his body, of its limitations and its
strengths. While developing this awareness, he can learn
many other things as well if he is invited to act them out, instead of having them explained to him abstractly.

As I've pointed out earlier, children are naturally inclined
to play games of "Let's Pretend." Acting out stories, working

out situations by having Jimmy stand here, Mary over there, and you somewhere, too, as part of the story, with everyone actually going through the parts, will make a much deeper impression on their minds than simply talking things out with them.

I am not much in favor of carrying this thought to its logical conclusion of walking the child through *every* lesson, or having him act it out with his body. One might in the present context, for instance, easily leap to the idea of teaching numbers, or the alphabet, by drawing great designs on the floor and having the child trace their outlines by walking along them. Never in later life, however, will he be likely to have to pace these things out with his feet. Most probably, he will always work with them with his hands and fingers.

The system used when I was a child was, I think, more realistic. Moreover, it, too, made use of the body—but of the hands, not the feet. We were given letters and numbers traced out on a page in sandpaper, and asked to follow these tracings with our fingers.

Another excellent way of teaching children through the use of their bodies is to involve them in simple dramatic presentations, with a minimum of words and a maximum of action. A suggestion: Give them the freedom to have fun, even if it disturbs the plot.

Dance movement can be an excellent means both of teaching bodily coordination and of developing "light" attitudes in the mind.

Any upward movement of arms, head, or torso can be used to suggest a rising awareness, and any downward movement to suggest heaviness of mind and feeling.

Children might be encouraged, when dancing, to concentrate more attention on their shoulders, arms, and hands, and correspondingly less on their lower limbs.

The major focus of many dances is on the lower part of the body: the hips, legs, and feet. In normal life these parts receive considerably less attention; their role is a supporting one. Normally, when people express their feelings or ideas physically, isn't it natural for them to use their arms and hands? It seems therefore right, in the consciousness-raising dances to which I am referring, to keep the lower limbs more in their natural, supportive role.

I am not suggesting always choreographing children's dances. Spontaneity should be encouraged as much as possible. Why not, rather, give names to various dance movements that will suggest of themselves the kinds of gestures intended?

One dance, for example, might be called, "Scattering Flowers."

Another, "Sharing the Sunlight."

Another, "Making Rainbows."

Still another, "Waking up the World."

"Trees Dancing" could make a delightful and unusual dance. So also, "Offering," and "Catching the Rain."

One dance, in which the legs and feet would receive full and enthusiastic play, might be called, "Stalking an Opportunity."

An important point to remember, I think, is not to suggest dances that the child might come to mock later on in life. For by such ridicule the whole system could be damaged. "Birds in Flight," for example, might be a perfectly good dance exercise, provided the birds visualized were large, soaring birds with wide wing spans and a calm beauty. If, however, the children should set themselves to flapping and hopping about like sparrows, they might have a good laugh at the time, but in later years they might remember the scene in all its absurdity, and tell their friends, "All I remember is, we used to hop madly about like a bunch of silly birds!" Impressions stored up at a young age often linger on in the memory as caricatures.

One means of using physical movement to impart other important lessons, along with body coordination, is through painting and color drawing. An excellent practice would be to get a class, in cooperation with the teacher, to paint story scenes together, each child designing a different part of the scene.

Colors are important to children. Drawings should always, therefore, if possible, be done in color. Children can also be made aware of the effect on their feelings of different colors, and of different shades of color. They can be helped to see, for example, how they themselves may choose to use a preponderance of red when they feel angry or resentful, and blue when they feel passive or calm.

The purer the color, the "lighter" and more expanded, usually, its influence on the mind. A teacher might get children to look into the rainbow prism of lights in a crystal; even to imagine themselves moving about in a magical world of rainbow hues. At this point, the teacher might invent for them a story, perhaps of a child entering such a world and having wonderful adventures with beings and with beautiful objects of radiant light.

A game that might also be played could be called, "Cheering up Colors." For this game, the children could be invited to take dull, unhappy hues and make them pure, bright, and happy.

Music and sound are important parts of a child's up-bringing. But what kind of music? What kinds of sound?

Much of modern popular music has repeatedly been demonstrated to have a harmful effect on the nervous system. The heavy beat of rock music is so deleterious that even plants have been known to send out tendrils in an opposite direction from the loudspeakers that were blaring it forth, as though the plants wanted desperately to escape their boxes! On the other hand, when classical music was played continuously, the plants reversed their direction and sent out tendrils that embraced the loudspeakers!

One can't expect to change a whole culture (if culture is the *mot juste*), but one can, at least, speak one's mind to anyone willing to listen.

The beat of much modern popular music is, in fact, contractive and heavy. It is ego affirming, not ego expansive. It takes the mind downward. There are few sights stranger or more incongruous, or less attractive, than a little child stamping its feet and writhing about to the violent music of a rock band. Naturally, children find an appeal in this kind of music, for it affirms their egos, which is already their natural center. But is this affirmation wholesome?

Much of modern popular music works directly contrary to any serious effort to bring children to maturity.

Music plays a vitally important role in life, and therefore in education. By rhythm and melody the mind can be inspired with devotion, or fired to risk life in battle; softened to sentiments of kindness and love; tickled to laughter, soothed to relaxation; or kindled to anger and violence.

One popular song years ago, called "Gloomy Sunday," was actually banned from the air waves. Too many people, having heard it, were committing suicide.

It has even been found that lessons learned against a background of baroque music, which has roughly sixty beats to the minute, register more deeply in the mind.

A delightful song in the movie, "The Sound of Music," has the von Trappe children singing a melody while naming the notes, thus: "Sol do la fa mi do re, sol do la ti do re do." I've never heard of children actually being taught to sing this way in school, but it's a wonderful idea. For, by thus naming the notes, they quickly learn them well enough to recognize them in any sequence.

Instead of the usual sequence, however,—"Do re mi fa sol la ti (or si) do"—children might enjoy it more if they named familiar things, and didn't merely utter meaningless sounds. "Sol," moreover,—the fifth note of the scale as it is normally sung—is a slightly clumsy syllable when followed by certain of the other notes: "sol re," for example, or "sol mi."

What about these sounds for the major scale: "Day, lark, rose, tree, moon, night, sea, day"? They flow well together in any sequence, and bring the notes more to life. In-between notes (the sharps in the *C* scale) might be named as they are here in parenthesis: "Day (break), lark (song), rose, tree (leaf), moon (ray), night (cloud), sea, day." These incidentals would, of course, help only those children who were already fairly well grounded in music.

Thus, the above melody would be sung: "Moon day night tree rose day lark, Moon day night sea day lark day."

Games of imagination might be played with individual notes, and also with groups of notes.

Nature provides endless opportunities for expanding the awareness of children. A game with great possibilities might be called, "Tuning in to Nature." The children are taken out of doors, and, perhaps standing around a tree, asked to suggest what they might learn from the tree: Strength, firmness of purpose, and so on. They are then asked to tune in to the tree, and to draw from it these virtues.

A fascinating book on this subject is Joseph Cornell's *Sharing Nature with Children.* *

An excellent practice, too, would be for the children to tune in to one another: to strive to *feel* qualities in their schoolmates that could prove helpful to themselves. They could even be encouraged to bless one another. In these ways, their natural childish tendency to scoff at one another could be tempered with charity.

They could also be invited to make garlands of wild flowers and garland one another, the teacher, and perhaps even children and teachers from other classrooms.

Thus, in all ways the children may be educated to respond to life with the best that is in them, and to develop, each one to his own highest potential.

---

*Ananda Publications, Nevada City, California.

17

The Feeling Years

MANY OF THE TECHNIQUES AND PRINCIPLES suggested in the last chapter can be carried through effectively into the later school years. The first three grades, especially, can be used to develop and refine everything this book has suggested for the pre-school years.

Moreover, it isn't at all the case that, with the end of those first six years, the method of teaching through body awareness may now be abandoned. In various ways, in fact, teaching through body movement should be continued throughout the years of formal education, and will prove useful throughout life. For every mental attitude has its counterpart in physical positions or gestures. The body and the mind are forever interactive.

What we must do, then, is not abandon one emphasis for another, as we shift from one six-year stage to the next. The first stage, rather, must serve as a foundation upon which the second stage of the building can be built. The second, in its turn, makes possible the third. And so on. Each progressive stage only raises the building higher; it doesn't call for a shift elsewhere, and the construction of a new building.

The first three years of grade school, especially, will call for a fuller development of the techniques suggested for the pre-school years, with the addition of a greater emphasis on emotional development and inspiration.

During the second three years of grade school, the teaching can become less concrete, and more abstract. The child's mind will now be more adept at handling concepts *as* concepts, rather than as images that must be acted out physically in order to be understood.

The emphasis throughout this six-year phase of education should be on teaching through the feelings and emotions, and on developing the finer feelings. For it is during these years that the child can begin seriously to control and direct his emotions, instead of merely letting them rule him.

Many thinking people, raised in our emotionally arid society, consider it quite enough merely to be able once again to *express* their feelings. "Get in touch with your feelings" was the advice making the rounds a few years ago. (And never mind if those feelings happened to be destructive.) Partly, the idea was that, by recognizing them, one would be able to change them. And partly it was that, by expressing them, one would be able to release them.

Major changes in people's lives, however, have not been reported to result from this system. Simple mental recognition of a problem hasn't been found to provide the requisite energy for banishing the problem. Worse still, as we've seen earlier in this book, *too much* mental recognition, and the intellectual conceptualization that such recognition entails, often actually robs people of the energy necessary for practical action.

Simply to give vent to a poisonous emotion, moreover, is by no means a permanent cure. The very technique is interestingly reminiscent of the practice of bloodletting by leeches in earlier, primitive medicine.

Granted, one may feel a temporary release after screaming with impotent exaggeration such maledictions as, "I want to kill my father!"—or weeping with helpless abandon for all the sorrows one has endured in life. Any such release, however, is short-lived. For there is always in this emotional "bloodletting" the thought, "*I* want," or "*I* grieve"—that sturdy thread by which the supposedly exorcised feeling remains unalterably bound to the ego.

It is difficult enough even for adults to escape their emotional problems by the mere act of facing them. But adults, at least, have other frames of reference by which to reduce any given emotion to its relative insignificance. Children have no such broadened perspective. They suffer from what might be termed emotional tunnel vision. Any feeling presently endured is likely to comprise their entire present definition of reality.

Simply put, children have no need to "get in touch with their feelings." They already live in their feelings. They have no need to affirm their negative feelings. Any such affirmation will only give strength to those feelings. Nothing will be gained from forcing them to suppress their feelings. What they need, instead, is to learn how to *channel* their feelings in positive directions.

One classic example of society's effort to suppress feelings, rather than rechannel them, is the common admonition, "Boys don't cry." What's wrong with crying, for heaven's sake? *Of course* a boy should cry, if he feels like it. Strength doesn't lie in the suppression of tears. It lies in the ability to redirect negative feelings.

127

It *is* weakness, on the other hand, not to be able to redirect them. And it feeds that weakness to show a boy too much pity. Show enough to let him know that you understand, but then, instead of merely trying to get him not to cry, try to get him to redirect his feelings in some new and positive direction—preferably one that is relevant to what he has been crying about, rather than urging him simply to "Come on and play outside."

We've examined in some detail in earlier chapters the importance of helping a child to raise his consciousness, and—almost synonymously—to expand it. He could be taught to do both, quite literally, as a means of redirecting his feelings.

First, you might urge him to sit up straight; to look upward; to do a little deep breathing.

Then, get him to think in a more expanded way: for instance, to see the situation from the other's point of view; or to see it as small, or temporary, in terms of his own broader realities; to be fair; to look upon the other fellow as needing his help and understanding.

It is important not to belittle his feelings. This is what creates harmful repressions. Try simply, instead, to get him to see his feelings in a broader perspective. Thus, you may reduce their importance in his own eyes.

It will be helpful also to teach the children the ability to abstract feelings and personality traits from their own, and from others', total reality. They can be helped to see that moodiness, for example, is not an essential characteristic of even the moodiest child; that we are not our personality traits, but something deeper, and that we can change those traits without, in the process, losing something of ourselves.

It will help the child very much to realize that being moody or angry doesn't define *him* as a moody or angry person. The possession of this psychological tool will make it considerably easier for him to change.

One way to teach such abstraction might be, first, through simple arithmetic addition and subtraction. Take, for example, two apples; then two more apples. Together they make four apples. Do the same thing with oranges. The result in each case is the same. The essential thing, then, in this addition is not the objects used, whether apples or oranges. It is the two-ness of them, which becomes, with addition, a four-ness. Both qualities have nothing to do with whether they are apples or oranges.

The same principle might then be applied to such abstractions as lightness and heaviness. Cotton, for example, as it grows on the plant is light and fluffy. In a ship's sail, however, it is condensed, and therefore heavy. Lightness or heaviness, then, are abstractions. An object may manifest one or the other of these properties without being defined by either of them. Iron, for example, will sink in water. In this context, therefore, it is heavy. But it will float in mercury, which fact, in this context, makes it light.

Study the lives of great people. Show how they *developed* heroism, courage, kindness; they weren't necessarily born with these qualities. Show also how, by repeated acts of selfishness, people can *become* mean, "heavy," and miserable.

By this means, the child can be taught to believe in his own ability to change, and also to separate others, in his own mind, from their faults: "to hate the sin," as the saying goes, "but not the sinner."

To help him to overcome a tendency to judge others, it may be emphasized to him that a person develops in himself any trait that he concentrates on, even if he concentrates on seeing it in others. Thus, if there is any quality that he hates in another child, and if he mentally judges that child for that quality, he will attract the same quality to himself. He should try to help others, therefore, and not condemn them, if only because by so doing he will help himself.

It may also be possible to help him see that he never hates qualities in others if there isn't some hint of that quality in himself. Thus, he can turn impetuous judgment of others into a tool of self-understanding, and of self-transformation.

Stories of great men and women are always inspiring. During the six-year stage that is being considered here, moreover, they have the greatest impact, and can actually help mold the child's entire future development.

It is a pity merely to entertain children with frivolous and meaningless tales, when the civilizations of history have produced such an abundance of worthwhile fables, allegories, and true episodes that make wonderful reading, and that are by turns amusing, witty, inspiring, and beautiful—everything, in short, that any story for children may aspire to be.

These also are the years of opportunity for learning something about the arts: painting, sculpture, music; and for getting a taste of the sheer romance of great scientific discovery.

Children at this time can be taught the difference between the right and wrong use of their physical senses.

The eyes, for example, should be trained to see beauty and truth, not ugliness and falseness. The ears should be trained to concentrate on absorbing goodness; on hearing kind words, beautiful sounds, and beautiful music; and not on absorbing depressing news, unkind words, negative judgments about others, ugly sounds, and ugly music. To repeat, we become what we concentrate on.

The tongue should be trained, similarly, to enjoy wholesome food, and to utter kind speech. The sense of touch should be disciplined to become one's servant, instantly obedient to the will, and not to revel in physical sensations to the extent of enslaving one to them. The sense of smell should be awakened to the fresh fragrance of flowers, herbs, and forest scents, and not be allowed to accustom itself only to the stale smells of exhaust fumes, cigarette smoke, and air-conditioned rooms.

The imagination should be trained also. A well developed, healthy imagination is the spring from which flows the creativity of genius. Visualizations can be offered the children to stimulate their imagination.

For instance: "Imagine yourself living in a forest. What is the forest like? Are you afraid there, or happy? Build yourself a home in the forest. What kind of a home would you like to build? Is it in a clearing, or in the deep woods?

"Think of the animals in the forest. Are they your friends? Or are you afraid of some of them?

"See yourself walking in forest paths. Whom do you meet there? Is it an animal, or a person? If it's a person, does he or she smile to see you? Have you done something to make him smile? If not, is there something you can do to make him smile?

131

"Imagine a pond in the forest. In the middle of this pond there is a small island. And on the island is a cup, resting on an ivory pedestal. What does the cup look like? Describe it. Does it contain something good to drink? What is the drink?

"Now, think of the cup as containing a wonderful, amber liquid, bubbling with energy and happiness. Drink this liquid. Suddenly, everything in the forest becomes cheerful, peaceful, and beautiful—full of sunshine and hope.

"Call all your friends—children, grown-ups, animals—to come and enjoy this magical drink with you. Ask them to join you in walking through this magical forest."

Countless similar exercises might be used to stimulate the children's imaginations. These exercises can become the themes for whatever subsequent paintings they create.

Children need to learn to *practice* cheerfulness—to be helped, in other words, to see that cheerfulness isn't only a mood that one feels when things go right; that one must work consciously at being cheerful under all circumstances.

Affirmations should become, during this second six-year stage of life, an important part of the child's daily routine, especially affirmations repeated with the movements suggested in Chapter 9.

In the first six years, many children will be more adept at appreciating music than at creating it. By the second six years, however, most of them should be ready for some sort of creativity. Those with sufficient talent could be invited to sing choral pieces together, to practice the Suzuki method of playing the violin, and in other ways to develop their musical sense.

Those with a talent for dancing could be encouraged to interpret music through dance, after they've been shown how different kinds of music correspond to different feelings in the heart.

Wholesome habits should be inculcated: cleanliness, a sense of neatness and order, even-mindedness, contentment, truthfulness, a cooperative spirit, servicefulness, responsibility, and respect toward others (especially toward one's elders).

Exercises can be used to help the child to become centered in himself—not self-centered, which is something very different, but restful and relaxed at his own inner center. Certain yoga postures are excellent for developing this awareness, with their gentle stretches left, right, forward, and back, always returning after each stretch to a position of rest in the middle.

Concentration, too, is vitally important in the child's development. Concentration is commonly associated with knit eyebrows and mental tension, but true concentration has nothing to do with strain. Rather, it means, simply, *absorption* in a thought or a perception, or in the search for a solution. Such an ability is vital for success of all kinds in life.

Daily, get the children to practice concentration for brief periods until it becomes a habit with them. Many techniques can be used effectively. Remind them, for example, how naturally they concentrate on anything that really interests them, like a good movie or an interesting story. Suggest that they look at an unmoving object with similar interest: a flower, a candle, the lights in a crystal. Remind them that they can create interest, and project it; that they needn't wait for interest to be awakened in them by objective stimulation; and that this interest, when focused, is all that is meant by concentration.

The highest feeling is that which lifts one in aspiration toward the highest reality. In this soaring aspiration, all lesser qualities become uplifted also, almost effortlessly. Not to teach children at this age, especially, to feel devotion seems to me the greatest disservice to them. It is to give them a body without the head; a large car with only a one-horse-power engine.

Devotion to what? I've given reasons already for everyone, even atheists, to accept the word *God,* each according to his own understanding.

I am reminded here of an encounter that I had, years ago, with a young man who was aggressively atheistic. I could get nowhere with him in my efforts to broaden his understanding of God as a universal concept.

Some time later that afternoon I offered him and a few others rides to wherever they wanted to go. A teenage girl in the car made the statement, apropos of nothing that I remember, that she didn't believe in love. After we'd let her off at her home, the self-styled atheist turned to me wonderingly.

"Can you imagine that?" he exclaimed: "Not believing in love!"

"And you call yourself an atheist?" I replied.

18

The Willful Years

THE IMMEDIATE INSPIRATION for this book was a dream I had. A group of aggressive teenage boys had surrounded me arrogantly. I wasn't afraid, but I do recall feeling a deep concern for them.

Toward the end of the dream, we were all walking up a street, talking together—they, lurching along in the self-conscious manner of so many teenagers. And I remarked, "Doesn't it seem that life should offer us something really worth living for? Surely kindness and friendship are worth more than being considered important? And isn't happiness something worth striving for, rather than something to reject as impossible?"

"That's right!" they exclaimed a little sadly. "It's what we all want."

And I felt their own deep intrinsic worth, their sense of innocence betrayed by an upbringing that had stripped them of everything in which they might have been able to believe.

The problems of modern education exist at all levels, but they surface into the full sunlight during the teenage years—the third stage of maturity.

It is, as I've already stated, during this six-year stage that the child feels a more pressing need to test his will power. It isn't that he won't test it sooner, any more than a child during his first six years of developing bodily awareness won't express emotion. (As I remarked, the chances are, during those years, that he'll express little else!)

A child of strong natural will power will show an inclination to express himself willfully from the start. However, just as the best time for learning to control the emotions is during the second six-year phase, so also the best time for consciously developing will power is during the third of these phases, up to the age of eighteen.

Idealism, for example, develops naturally, with only a little encouragement, during the six years preceding one's twelfth birthday. But this tends to be an idealism more sentimental than practical. With the adolescent's dawning instinct for expressing will power, there comes the inclination to put idealism into practice. Such, at least, is the opportunity of adolescence. Alas, it proves all too often an opportunity missed.

For with the onset of puberty, there comes a growing preoccupation with oneself *as* a self—as an ego, separate and distinct from all other egos. The child's developing sexual awareness forces upon him a major redefinition of his priorities—of how he sees himself, how he relates to others, and what he expects from life.

Sexual awareness tends to pull the adolescent's energy and consciousness downward, toward spiritual "heaviness." This directional flow, coupled with his natural self-preoccupation, is contractive in consciousness, resulting in deep psychological pain for the child. If, moreover, his natural mental inclination is upward, this unaccustomed downward flow brings him also a period of spiritual confusion.

With sexual awareness also, on the other hand, there comes a sense of potential inner power, of creativity, which, if not directed into right channels, may easily be diverted into destructive ones.

Should ever the mind be brought to a repudiation of the idealism it held as a younger child, it may reject idealism altogether, and employ all its creative power cynically in this purely negative act.

How is an adolescent to be encouraged not to lose his early idealism? Advantage can actually be taken of the changes that take place in his body and psyche with the advent of puberty.

His awakening sense of inner power can be directed toward making his ideals practical, instead of rejecting them negatively as impractical. Early dreams must now be translated into dynamic action—refined, perhaps, in their definition, but not cynically abandoned.

Adolescence needs a cause—or, better still, an abundance of causes. It needs something to *do*. It is like dynamite: if exploded heedlessly above the ground, it may only destroy; but if exploded carefully underground, it may create roads over which others will someday pass.

Adolescence, rightly approached and understood, is a wonderful time of life, rich with some of the greatest opportunities that a person will ever know. The important thing to understand is the adolescent's need for *action,* not theory.

Physical discipline is important. So also is any call to good deeds without personal reward—the greater the self-sacrifice entailed, the better, provided, obviously, that the child's well-being isn't endangered.

Self-reliance needs to be stressed in numerous ways, including camping out in the wilderness, boy scout activities, tests of personal endurance, and the like.

Other tests can be given the teenager for developing his will power. If he feels a cold coming on, for example, he might try casting it out of his body by will power. (This can be done quite effectively, provided the cold is caught at an early enough stage.)

He can be encouraged to test the power of positive thinking—on his own life, on the lives of others, and on objective circumstances. A positive, strong will power has been shown to be capable of influencing many things, especially one's own inner consciousness, for the better.

The teenager, so often pampered by a worried adult population, actually needs just the opposite treatment: *challenges!* the sheer dare to do better than he imagines possible. Of course, he must be *drawn* forward, never yanked. The challenges must spring out of his own higher self; they must not be imposed upon him unnaturally by the excessive ambition of his elders.

What is to be done about the wrong directions that so many teenagers have already taken? It is all very well to approach adolescence as a wonderful time of life, provided we can begin working on the adolescent from the age of twelve. But what about vast numbers of older adolescents, who have already developed strongly negative behavioral patterns? Is there any hope for them?

Indeed there is, though admittedly it won't be easy. All of the above guidelines apply. Negativity must be recognizcd and dealt with. *Faith,* however, in the children's potential must be the underlying attitude, and never an acceptance of their own negative self-image.

The important thing is to realize that most children do want true values. Their negativity is, for the most part, only symptomatic of their disillusionment at being given nothing positive in which to believe.

Two courses only have the potential to turn the currently destructive atmosphere into a constructive one. One—but this one can't be produced to order—could be a spiritual renascence of some deep, experiential kind. The other would be the opposite of the usual impulse to sidestep or pamper: firm, though loving, discipline.

I say *loving,* because without love, discipline won't work. I'm not recommending the boot camp type of training. This would only undermine the good work suggested for the six-to-twelve years, the feeling years.

But it might help for people to understand the merit even of stern discipline, lest loving discipline come to be equated with feeble smiles and futile remonstrances.

In the Swiss army, some years ago, there was a regiment consisting of the lowest and roughest elements in society, men who categorically refused all discipline. Its members arose in the morning whenever they felt like it; showed up for drill, or not, as they chose; talked back insolently to their officers; and made it abundantly clear that they had only contempt for a law that made it mandatory for every adult male in Switzerland to serve his time in the army.

All the officers were afraid of them. None had the courage to enforce discipline. And then, at last, a new colonel was placed in charge of them.

This man decided he simply wasn't going to put up with such slovenly behavior. His cure? To discipline them more severely than any other regiment in the army. Brother officers waited with bated breath for him to be shot in the back.

But the regiment accepted his no-nonsense approach— so much so that in a few months they developed into the best disciplined group in the whole army, and the unit with the highest esprit de corps.

As long as parents and teachers are afraid to be firm, poor discipline, and the many negative attitudes that result from it, will be endemic in the schools.

Too many adults, unfortunately, are more concerned with being loved than with loving. If they really loved, they would give the children what they really need. During adolescence, the child's will power needs to be tested and strengthened, not shrugged off, merely, as a test for his elders.

* * *

One of the most sensitive areas of adolescence is the ever-present possibility of failure. This threat is, to be sure, never far absent even from the adult. But in the adolescent, the slightest social gaff, the most trivial manifestation of gaucheness assumes nightmare proportions in oneself, and unforgettably ludicrous dimensions in his companions.

Failure must be addressed, therefore, not shunned as too embarrassing a topic for open discussion.

In fact, failure is forever intrinsic to success. Anyone who never fails in life by the same token never succeeds.

Failure is an instrument of learning. Every failure, if rightly understood, can be a stepping stone to success.

Indeed, it is never wise to say, "I've failed." Say, rather, "I haven't yet succeeded." For the repeated thought of failure is an affirmation which eventually weakens the will. But the repeated thought of success, even in the face of continual failure, is an affirmation which *must,* eventually, produce the desired results.

The adolescent must be shown that the person who never fails has, in a sense, already failed. A career without failures is the mark of one who has never dared. And great success comes to him alone who dares greatly. No matter how many times one fails, victory is assured him whose courage never flags. Indeed, a courageous spirit can squeeze victory of a kind even from crushing defeat.

As Paramhansa Yogananda used to say of the spiritual search: "A saint is a sinner who never gave up!"

The adolescent should be taught the importance of self-control; and of *self*-discipline, not merely outward discipline. It will help him to fast occasionally; to go for periods of time without his favorite foods; to do things against which his desire for ease rebels; to do things for others with the deliberate purpose of overcoming his own natural egoism.

Servicefulness is a wonderful quality, too little appreciated in this age of aggressive self-affirmation. There is joy in the expansive consciousness of forgetting self in the affirmation of a larger good.

Affirmations, too, many of which have been suggested already, can be an excellent tool of self-discipline and self-transformation.

An excellent book on behavior is Dale Carnegie's *How to Win Friends and Influence People*. The title may sound manipulative, but the book is in fact an invaluable guide for anyone who wants to learn how to live sensitively in the company of others.

One of the pitfalls of adolescence is lack of enthusiasm. An excellent way of overcoming this lack is to get the young person to express enthusiasm outwardly with great vigor, even if inwardly he feels none. The greater the expression of will, the greater—surprising as it seems—the flow of energy to succeed at whatever one sets oneself to accomplish.

Young people of "light spiritual gravity" often find themselves at a disadvantage during adolescence, owing to the aggressive emphasis placed on the ego by so many of their fellows. The ego, to many at that age, seems all-important, a thing to be affirmed constantly, and thrust out at others as though daring them to match one's own degree of self-importance. Often, or so it seems at that age, the greater the egotist, the more powerful, magnetic, and successful the youth. Hence the popularity of football heroes, and the comparative obscurity, all too frequently, of idealists.

Only later in life does it begin to become evident that we are all part of a much greater reality, and that attunement with that reality is needed for us to accomplish the really great things in life. The great scientists, for example, have never been those who boasted to the universe, "You'll do as *I* say!" They have been those, rather, who said humbly, "Help me to understand what it is *you* are saying."

A friend of mine and his family visited California several

months ago. I and several others took them to Disneyland, where, for one of the rides, we hired small boats, each one big enough to seat a couple of people.

The boats had what appeared to be steering wheels, but what were in fact dummies. Most of us quickly discovered that no matter how we turned them, the boats continued on their own course, determined by a system of underwater tracks.

At one point, my companion and I saw our friend and his wife passing us by another channel. As we hailed them, his wife tried to get him to call out something to us.

"Don't disturb me!" he cried, tensely. "Don't you see, I'm steering this boat! If I don't, we'll hit those rocks over there."

What a laugh his daughters had on him afterward!

And how similar is the case of many people, who imagine that in all things they are the doers, and fail to realize how many things in life simply can't be controlled, and had best, therefore, be understood and accepted.

The lesson of adolescence, ultimately, should be to strengthen, not the ego, but the will power—as a stepping stone towards true maturity. This stepping stone should be seen with humility, as but one of several stones, by crossing all of which the adolescent will be able not only to understand, but to feel himself part of, a reality greater than his own.

19

The Thoughtful Years

W HEN YOUNG PEOPLE TURN EIGHTEEN, they seem, as it were suddenly, to enjoy sitting about in little groups discussing politics, philosophy, religion, the meaning of life, and other abstract subjects—or, alternatively, recent and future business trends, or the latest scientific theories. The change in their behavior isn't due so much to new methods of education, for at college the basic classroom set-up isn't all that much different from what it was in high school. Whatever changes there are, rather, in the educational method are due more probably to an attempt to adjust to changes in the attitudes of the students themselves.

At this time of life, the young person begins to appreciate the truth in those famous words of the English poet, Bulwer-Lytton: "The pen is mightier than the sword." For with the unfolding of his intellect, he enters the fascinating world of ideas, and discovers in them a power far greater than mere brute force.

The important thing at this age, as we have seen earlier, is to teach young people to reason clearly, rather than merely cleverly. For the intellect can be used with almost equal skill to clarify situations or to obscure them; to find positive, helpful solutions to problems, or to block every hint of a worthwhile solution.

Reason is a tool, merely: a path, not a goal. The student should be taught to use it rightly, lest, like an inexpertly used power tool, it slip and cut him.

For truth simply *is*. It cannot be created; it cannot be distorted; it cannot be denied. One may play with it as shrewdly as one likes; one may put on a superb show and convince the whole world. Truth always wins in the end. And lies, sooner or later, are always discredited and abandoned.

The student needs to be convinced of these realities by every means possible. For they are unalterable. Only by accepting them can he be certain to avoid the temptation to use reason's power erroneously.

How many times in history a person, or an entire nation, has insisted on a wrong course of action, and offered what seemed at the time the best possible reasons in support of this direction. Often, anyone believing differently was branded a heretic or a traitor.

And so, kings raised mighty armies to go off and fight useless crusades. Priests tortured and killed in God's name for the so-called "holy" inquisition. Thousands invested confidently in the illusory "South Sea Bubble." A nation enthusiastically endorsed the Nazi myth of "Aryan supremacy." And communists everywhere today subscribe to the typical partisan's definition of justice: Truth is that which advances the communist cause.

All who have ever tried to mold truth to their own liking, regardless of how many people they may have managed to convince, have failed ingloriously at last.

Truth alone wins, in the end.

In learning to reason wisely, the student should have emphasized to him the importance of always being willing to re-evaluate his first principles. His commitment should be, not to any idea about truth, nor to any mere definition of it, *but to truth itself.*

Thus, the student should be encouraged to develop a quality fundamental to clear insight: the willingness at once, and without the slightest attachment to any previous stand, to change his mind when confronted with facts which prove him to have been wrong.

Here is an excellent classroom exercise:

Get the class fully, even emotionally, committed to an idea, or to a course of action. Then prove to them that that idea or action is, after all, erroneous.

Get them into the habit of changing mental directions, when necessary, at a moment's notice; of always keeping the needle of their mental compass pointed toward the truth, and never toward any personal opinion, no matter how attractive an idea in their eyes.

Few scientists, even, are capable of divorcing reason from desire so completely. The ability to do so must be classed as one of the ego's real triumphs in the long quest for maturity. But although we may expect few students to free their mental processes enough to reason so clearly, no effort should be spared to make them aware of the advantages of this kind of thinking.

Take some—take *any*—universally held belief: the more emotional the students' commitment to it, the better. Many professors do something like this already. They'll take the belief in democracy, for example, and reinforce it with the usual arguments in its favor. Then they'll point out the flaws in this system of government—not, if they are wise, from a wish to undermine the students' faith in democracy, but rather to help them base their faith on honestly held reasons, and not on emotionally held, a priori assumptions.

A similar exercise: Get the students emotionally committed to some immediate *cause célèbre,* perhaps something on campus. And then see if they can be made to listen fairly to the arguments of the other side.

Again, this exercise: Teach them to *listen* to different points of view on many issues—to hear other people out with respect, and not with emotion; to appreciate other ways of reasoning than their own. Show them that it isn't enough, in any meaningful discussion, to convince oneself; that the way to convince others is to enter into their point of view, to understand it in its own context, and to answer them in their own terms.

An important point to teach students is that the only way to reason clearly is *to reason with non-attachment.* The person of clear intellect, in his willingness to accept the truth of a situation whatever it might be, finds himself able also to respect others' right to hold divergent opinions, no matter how patently fallacious, realizing as he does so that opinions (his own included) count for little or nothing anyway: Truth alone endures.

Non-attachment is supremely important in the search for truth. The important thing is to learn how to remain non-attached without becoming indifferent. This end can be accomplished by heartfelt dedication to truth itself.

Again, how is one to become non-attached? By always trying to separate what *is* from what merely seems to be.

147

Take a simple example: an advertisement for the popular beverage, "muddies," depicting a crowd of laughing, happy people drinking this deadly brew. Obviously, what the advertiser wants is to suggest that the crowd's happiness is due to the fact that it is drinking "muddies," or at least that a mood of happiness "with the gang" automatically induces the sympathetic desire for this product—that "muddies" is, to coin a term, a happiness-compatible drink.

The reality, probably, is that people drink "muddies" quite as often in a state of solitary gloom. Certainly, no such drink can ever produce happiness. For people are happy only from within themselves; it is after the fact that they project happiness onto external objects. Objects in themselves, including even—let's face it—"muddies," are always neutral in their effect, neither positive nor negative until so defined by the mind.

I have occasionally taken the opportunity to test this method for achieving non-attachment when seated in the dentist's chair—a difficult test, perhaps, but for that very reason the more instructive. What I've done is refuse to have my nerves deadened by Novocain, in order to try to separate myself by dispassion from the sensation of pain.

Here's how the process works: There is the sensation itself, which is basically neutral. And then there is the mental definition of it as pain. Further, there is the emotional reaction: "I dislike this sensation of pain."

Mentally detach yourself from the emotional reaction. Instead of concentrating on your dislike for the pain, concentrate on the simple, undefined sensation. If it is very painful, concentrate fully on the pain *as a sensation,* rather than on your pained reaction to the sensation.

Next, try to separate that sensation from your definition of it as painful. Tell yourself that it is only a sensation, and that, as such, it can be defined in various ways, and not only as painful. Whatever definition you give it, remember, will be your own mental projection onto the sensation.

Try, then, defining it in various other ways: as interesting; as noisy rather than painful; as an exercise in concentration.

Next, try not defining it at all.

I've had dentists actually sweating in sympathetic agony over me, while I myself sat back and, after a little effort at non-attachment, devoted the rest of the session to mentally working out problems I'd been facing in musical composition.

One method for the development of clear reasoning is the deliberate practice of sophistry. Students may be invited to compete in thinking up the largest number of arguments in support of some stand which everyone knows to be false. They can have great fun in the process, and will gradually train themselves to recognize specious reasoning whenever they are confronted with it seriously in life.

Take, as an example, the comic song from the musical "Oklahoma!": "I'm just a Girl Who Can't Say No." The words go, "Whatcha gonna do when a feller talks purdy... Whatcha gonna do: Spit 'n his eye?" Here, the young ladies in the audience are given, as the only reasonable alternative to flirting back, an act that would condemn them in everyone's eyes as uncivilized. Therefore, a girl should *of course* welcome flirting—from any feller at all!

Or take the criminal's oft-heard argument in support of crime: at least it teaches people to take greater care of their possessions.

I am not up on the history of sophistry, but I wonder whether it was not originally devised as an amusing technique for helping students of philosophy to protect themselves against the pitfalls of false reasoning, and not what it may have become only later: a method for winning people to error by false arguments.

Students should be shown the difference not only between true and false reasoning, but also between truth and fact. This is an important distinction, though one not often recognized.

A truth is that which is in harmony with all levels of reality, whereas a fact may pertain to only one such level.

For example: A person ill in bed may look quite as badly as he feels. It would be perfectly in consonance with the facts to tell him, "You look terrible!" But what would such a statement do to the poor fellow's efforts to recuperate?

Anyone making such a statement might justify it with the words, uttered in wide-eyed innocence, "But I only wanted to tell the truth." Statements like that can give truth a bad name! In fact, however, the statement wouldn't be true; it would merely be factual.

A truth, as I said, is that which is in harmony with all levels of reality, and not that which pertains to only one such level. A look at the above statement in this light shows that many levels of reality have been ignored: the patient's chances, given a little encouragement, of improving; the importance to his recovery of boosting his morale; the therapeutic value of affirming good health; even the somewhat abstract philosophical point that, on a deeper level of being, perfection, rather than imperfection, *is* the truth.

An important aspect of learning to reason correctly is to understand the difference between reason and discrimination.

A line of reasoning will be false if its premise is false. Often, however, reason alone is inadequate to the task of evaluating the merits of a premise. Hence the need for discrimination.

Take the argument: Man is inherently evil, and should therefore always be approached defensively. Reason tells us that *if* mankind is inherently evil, then perhaps indeed he should be approached defensively. That is, from this premise, the stated conclusion may well follow logically.

Reason, however, is not adequate for determining in the first place whether mankind really is evil or not. One would need another premise, perhaps, indeed, several of them, and perhaps a whole series of logical deductions, to arrive at a conclusion that would probably not be convincing anyway.

What is needed is another faculty: intuition, held in a state of reason, but dependent besides on clear inner feeling: discrimination, in short. One may scoff at this concept, but intuitive discrimination is a faculty we all use. It is one, besides, on which the greatest geniuses have relied constantly. Without it, mankind would be incapable of arriving at clear answers on virtually any issue of importance.

For what is the alternative? If we rely on logic alone, we find ourselves entangled in so many strands of reason that, eventually, it becomes impossible to proceed a step further.

The human mind is ever forced to simplify, if it is to function at all. An interesting definition of genius, indeed, might be the capacity to reduce to simple terms concepts that to most people seem complex.

Reason, when not held in check and guided by other faculties of the mind, proliferates with such wild abandon that, far from clarifying, it merely confuses. One way in which it creates confusion is to draw the mind so forcibly to a line of logic that one forgets even to examine the premise.

When reasoning, people often accept premises without discrimination simply because the premises don't enter the flow of logic, and often are impossible to test logically. Once, moreover, the habit is established of accepting premises "for the sake of argument," reasoning based on those premises is often not examined closely enough, either.

Take the conclusion to the above argument: Man is evil, and *therefore* should always be approached defensively. There may, in fact, be alternative ways of approaching him. Logical conclusions arc too often arrived at with too facile a certainty, and with disdain for other logical possibilities.

I am reminded here of the story of a certain brahmin who is said to have told a Western archeologist: "In all the excavations conducted in India, not a single electric wire has ever been discovered. This *proves* that in ancient India they had the wireless!"

No line of reasoning is safe that is not checked constantly against the facts, or, alternatively, against actual experience. Otherwise it may be possible to argue for almost any absurdity with seemingly flawless logic—as someone once actually tried to do with me, beginning with the premise that guns are phallic symbols and used only to sublimate sexual desire. He concluded that the best way, therefore, to banish war would be to encourage the widespread practice of homosexuality.

The experience, of course, against which to test such an assertion would be a simple investigation into the relative non-violence of homosexuals, or, for that matter, of exuberantly self-expressive heterosexuals. It seems safe to predict—considering historic accounts of famous warriors—that no such correlation would be found.

And how is one to discriminate regarding the validity of a given premise? Again, where possible, by experience.

Experience, for example, suggests many instances to prove that mankind, while perhaps inherently evil, is also inherently good—in fact, a mixture of both good and evil.

But does experience resolve the still deeper question of what, really, is good or evil—or, for that matter, what is right or wrong? Not so easily.

Discrimination can only proceed from an awareness of reality on many levels. Here is an example:

There were, in a certain university a few years ago, two groups of aspiring writers. Both groups were reported to be equally talented. One consisted of only women students; the other, of only men. The goal of each group was to help its members to develop their writing skills.

The men sought to accomplish this end by criticizing one another's papers. Anything submitted was analyzed carefully and at length for its flaws.

The women, on the other hand, sought to help one another by offering positive encouragement.

Of the men's group, not a single member went on after graduation to become a professional writer. But of the women's group, several later achieved fame as authors, editors, and reporters.

In both cases, intellectual analysis was used skillfully.

The men, however, used it to address the single level of reality that appeared pertinent to them at the time: the manuscripts. The women used it to address other levels as well. Both groups may have reasoned equally clearly, but they certainly didn't do so with equal effectiveness.

A worthwhile exercise would be to set up *positive* encounter groups.

We are familiar with the negative type of encounter group, where people sit about and tear one another to psychological shreds. The tradition is not new. Christian monks and nuns have made it a practice for centuries to gather together and draw one another's attention—in "charity"—to their spiritual shortcomings.

Why not, then, a new kind of encounter group: one where students offer one another *really* charitable suggestions for how to strengthen their positive qualities? In the process each would assist, even without being aware of doing so, the development of such qualities in himself.

Young people need to learn how to reason not only well, but effectively—or, to put it another way, appropriately. There are times for analysis—for separating and distinguishing things from one another. And there are times for putting things together—for making them work together as a harmonious whole. The intellect must learn when to analyze, and when to unite; when to function on a level of abstraction, and when, on one of encouragement and compassion

The intellect must be used to discern that there are, in fact, many levels of reality.

Maturity, as we have said, means the ability to relate to other realities than one's own. In human affairs, then, it means the ability to relate to *human* realities, and not merely to the things with which human beings happen to be involved.

In the above instances, it was the writers, especially, who needed developing—the people *as* writers; less so, their manuscripts. The men failed because they treated one another primarily as producers of manuscripts, not as people.

Discrimination is the ability to perceive various levels of reality at once, and to *sense* which among them, in any given situation, are of primary importance.

Discrimination is impossible without humility, for it demands an understanding that truth exists already, that it cannot be created, but only perceived.

As a part of such humility, students should be taught respect for the insights of others, and above all for the longer traditions of the human race: those accepted verities which, throughout the ages, have spelled the difference between wisdom and ignorance.

More important even than valid traditions is the possibility of fresh, but valid, discovery. For in such freshness lies creativity, and in creativity lies self-expansion. Reason's definitions help one to rise from one level of understanding to another, but no definition can serve in place of the reality it defines. Thus, the student should be encouraged to be ready at any time to discard old definitions in favor of new, expanded vistas of reality.

20

The Curriculum

THREE CENTURIES AGO, there were certain people in England who wanted the freedom to worship as they chose. As pilgrims they came to the New World, and founded what was to become, a century later, the United States of America.

Their reason for leaving England was that the burden of tradition there made it difficult for them to establish themselves in a new identity. Their difficulty, probably, sprang not only from the persecution they endured, but also from the fact that it is never easy to follow new paths so long as one remains surrounded by old ways of living.

Jesus remarked that a prophet has no honor in his own country. It says much for his own greatness that it didn't occur to him to add that a prophet has a hard time *being* a prophet in his own country.

Young people with new dreams leave home to achieve them. Fritz Kreisler, the famous violinist, left Austria to attain greatness in America. His mother tried to prevent him. Years later he remarked, "If I had listened to her, I would not have become Fritz Kreisler."

Change, even under the most favorable of circumstances, is

seldom easy. It is even less so when pursued under the influence of old thought patterns.

A century after the arrival of the pilgrim fathers in America, and as the colonies began to prosper, it became increasingly evident that the freedom which the pilgrims had sought, and which remained the dream of subsequent immigrants, required still clearer definition. For a new spirit was growing here, one that could not flourish so long as the New World continued to be defined as a colony, merely.

It is not surprising that England felt challenged by this new spirit, and tried to suppress it. By the standards of a long tradition, much of what was going on in the colonies amounted to betrayal.

In fact, however, America simply needed a new self-identity. Only after the old traditions had been repudiated by means of the Revolution, and new ones established by the Constitution, could the new spirit become a real force in the world.

Often it happens that new ideas flourish only after they are placed in the context of a new system. In old contexts, the sheer weight of past habit tends to suffocate them.

Where the ideas in this book are concerned, no major revolution, obviously, is anticipated! Nevertheless, some thought must be given to the need for placing them in a new context. It may be that they will take root only in an altogether new school system.

One such school, or, rather, group of schools is already in existence. It will be described in the next chapter.

Best of all, of course, would be for these ideas to win acceptance directly into the general school system. But in this case, the ground will need to be prepared to receive them. And one step in this preparation would be the adoption of a new curriculum of studies.

*   *   *

The school curriculum as it now stands might, in fact, be adapted to the ideas contained in this book. But it is doubtful whether this adaptation would work. It would be like a heart transplant that is rejected by the body. Almost inevitably, transitional categories would tend to reassume their old definitions. Slowly, the customary designations— *The Sciences, Mathematics, Social Science, Languages, the Humanities*—would close their gates against this brash upstart, the "Education for Life" system. Or else, bit by bit, they would re-absorb the fresh principles of this new system into their old, theoretical approach.

A new curriculum may be difficult, in principle, to contemplate. Any education worthy of the name, after all, must instruct children in the basics of modern knowledge, and these basics include every one of the above categories of the curriculum. But in fact all that is really needed is a new set of designations for those categories. The curriculum itself need not in any way be abandoned, nor even drastically changed.

America, similarly, needed only to be redefined as a country, rather than as "the American colonies"—and well defined, too, through its Constitution—for it fully to assume its destined role.

Here, then, are suggestions for a new, and workable, curriculum. Be it noted that it includes all the standard academic subjects. The only difference is that it defines them in such a way as to invite, rather than merely tolerate, the inclusion of creative "Education for Life" principles as well.

* * *

The Sciences—one of the standard categories of study—is a lifeless designation, surely. It suggests method, rather than content, and conjures up images of test tubes in a laboratory, rather than the wonders of nature.

What about creating a new definition: *Our Earth—Our Universe?* This designation includes everything now being taught under the more sterile name, *The Sciences.* But it invites at the same time the consideration of a great deal more: a vision of the orderliness of the universe; an appreciation for the ecological balance of all life; a sense of awe before the universal mysteries which, as Einstein said, is the essence of scientific discovery.

The suggested designation invites students themselves to relate harmoniously to the universe around them—to feel themselves a part of everything, instead of being the merely intellectual observers of life.

Our Earth—Our Universe is a title that suggests a progressively expansive view of reality. It encourages students to see the particular in relation to the universal, and the immediate as a moment in vast eons of time.

The separate sciences, too, can thus be taught less as individual, compartmentalized disciplines, and more as a total reality revealed in its varied aspects. In this way, nature will assume for the student an over-all coherence which will be conducive to the basic goal of education itself: maturity. It is easier, after all, to relate to many realities when those realities are seen in meaningful relationship to one another.

One thing that ties the sciences together is the scientific method. In order, then, to show them also in meaningful relationship to other branches of knowledge, it may be explained how the scientific method—*hypothesis, tested by experiment*—can serve man in other aspects of his search for understanding. To accomplish this end, the scientific formula need only be restated as follows: *Belief, tested by experience.* In essence, these two formulae are the same.

Our Earth—Our Universe, as a general heading, would include these specific subjects: physics, astronomy, chemistry, biology, general science, botany, geology, and anatomy.

* * *

Another category of study might be designated, *Personal Development.* Under this heading would come a wide range of subjects, from physical to mental to spiritual development.

Physical development would include hygiene, diet, sex education, sports, and general physical education.

Mental development would include concentration, problem solving, how to develop the memory, secrets of balanced living, how to achieve and maintain inner centeredness, self-control, and joyful self-discipline.

Spiritual development would include secrets of happiness, and instruction in such attitudes as openness of heart and mind, truthfulness, non-attachment, calmness of feeling, willingness, servicefulness, and humility.

* * *

A third category might be designated, *Self-Expression and Communication.* This would include teachings, such as mathematics and grammar, that help one to achieve mental clarity.

Included here also would be such subjects as how to develop creativity, and how to be creative in different fields. Subjects might include the arts, interpretive dance, music composition, music interpretation, creative writing; and also instruction in how to develop more mundane, but perennially useful, skills such as carpentry, computer technology, public speaking, and salesmanship (to suggest as broad a sampling of studies as possible).

Students of self-expression should be taught the laws of success, and the difference between true success and success that is delusive.

They should be taught the importance of the human voice as a medium of self-expression; how to use the voice in speaking and in singing; how to develop its tones, and its emotional overtones, to the fullest; how to project the voice as a vehicle for thought and feeling, and how to project it to reach an audience.

Above all, they should be taught self-expression as a means of *communication,* and not merely as a means of self-imposition.

* * *

The next general category might be designated, *Understanding People*. This heading would include history, geography, psychology, a study of customs and beliefs in a diversity of cultures, and an evaluation of different mores in terms of what human beings themselves, everywhere, want most deeply from life.

* * *

The fifth general category in the curriculum might be designated, *Cooperation*. This heading is so named in order to give a positive emphasis to subjects that are normally studied with insufficient reference to their more human realities: languages, political science, economics, business.

Included here might be courses in such immediately helpful subjects as how to win friends and influence people (the title of Dale Carnegie's book); how to get along with others; how to find a suitable mate; secrets of a happy marriage; how to raise children; how to find a job; the importance of working *with* others, rather than against them; and the art of supportive leadership.

* * *

Thus, we have four subjects specifically directed toward "Education for Life" principles: Personal Development, Self-Expression and Communication, Understanding People, and Cooperation. And we also cover the field of the sciences with a title compatible with these principles.

There remains a need for one over-all subject with

which to tie them all together and give coherence to the entire system.

This sixth category might be designated, simply, *Wholeness.*

Under Wholeness would come such general topics as art and music *appreciation,* literature, philosophy, and religion. In teaching these subjects, constant reference ought to be made to the subjects studied under other headings. Thus, instruction in them will become instantly real and practical, and not merely, as it so often is in traditional schooling, abstract.

21

Ananda School

THE SYSTEM OF EDUCATION suggested in this book is more than a proposal: It is also a report. Many of the ideas contained here are already in practice. They have been refined over decades, including nearly twenty years of experience in a group of schools, from pre-school through high school, called the Ananda Schools—or, more usually, Ananda School.

Ananda School is small. It has not been widely publicized. Although unknown to a large public, however, it has already received recognition in educational circles.

Not long ago, a couple in Illinois inquired of several organizations in the eastern states whether they knew of a school that taught the art of living, as well as the standard curriculum. More than one organization replied that, for this purpose, the best school in America was Ananda School.

Another couple in Florida made a similar inquiry, and received the same answer.

At Ananda School, in other words, many of the principles suggested in this book have long been practiced, and their effectiveness to a great extent tested and proved.

A number of the ideas here suggested, however, represent new developments for Ananda School as well. What I have sought to do in these pages is re-evaluate our experience to date, and to see how what we've learned might be crystalized into a clear and coherent system, for the first time called "Education for Life."

This book seeks to address also the broader issue of education in America, with a view to exploring ways in which the presently established system in this country might be improved.

I mentioned, in Chapter 7, that it has fallen to me to found a community. This community was founded nearly twenty years ago. It is the larger entity of which Ananda School is a part. The community bears the same name as the school: Ananda.

Ananda is a Sanskrit word, meaning *Joy*. Miraculously, this community has actually managed to live up to its name. It is a notably joyful community! Ananda Village, with its various subsidiaries, numbers several hundred members, all of whom are dedicated to exploring the principles implicit in an education for life.

Ananda communities are as far-flung as California and Italy. The original and largest of these, Ananda Village, is situated on 700 acres in the foothills of the Sierra Nevada mountains of northern California, near the town of Nevada City.

Ananda Village is in fact, as its name implies, a village, not a commune. Its members live for the most part separately in their own homes. Some own their own businesses, and employ other members. Others work in businesses owned by the community.

Since its inception in 1967, Ananda Village has been prominent among new communities in the world.

Ananda School is an integral part of the life of the community. It is attended not only by the community's hundred or so children, but also by day and boarding students from the outside.

The goal of Ananda School is to teach children the art of living, while giving them in addition a conventional education. The principles taught here have been worked out through nearly two decades of trial and error on the part of the adults as well as of the children of the community.

Existing, as Ananda does, outside the mainstream of city and suburban life, we have yet remained identified with the broader culture around us. Spatial removal has enabled us to approach many of contemporary society's problems with freshness and creativity—even as the early pilgrim fathers did when they emigrated to the New World. What we have sought are answers that would be relevant to people everywhere, and not only to ourselves.

Our approach, then, has been one of positive affirmation. While to some extent withdrawing from the bustle of city life, we have never alienated ourselves from that life. Some of our newer experiments in constructive living, indeed, have been established in the cities. We *believe* in the underlying goodness of man, as we believe in our own underlying goodness. And we have been confident that it would be possible, by devoting ourselves creatively to the simple art of living, to find new and useful solutions to many of modern society's problems.

We have, moreover—so we believe—actually found a few solutions, some of which are contained in this book.

Ananda School was founded soon after our beginnings, as a natural response to the needs of the children in our community. We were fortunate from the start to have a few accredited teachers.

Accreditation in many professions, in fact, has long been one of Ananda's strengths. Community members presently include not a few professional people with high standing in their own fields. The problem, at first, was not so much how to create a school, but how to approach education afresh, from a standpoint of the Art of Living. None of us was satisfied with the presently accepted standards of education.

Studies were made by Ananda teachers of various progressive systems of education. We weren't committed to any dogma of education, but only to finding what would work best.

We were, however, committed to a certain premise: the firm conviction that a growing child needs to learn how to *live* in this world, and not merely how to find and hold a job; how to live wisely, happily, and successfully, according to his own deepest inner needs.

We were eager to learn from anyone who could teach us. Gradually, however, direct experience provided us with a clarity of our own. Life itself, as this book recommends, began superseding books as our teacher.

It was important to validate our evolving "Education for Life" system on a standard academic level as well. Our children needed to be able to compete adequately with children elsewhere in the country.

In fact, in nationwide exams Ananda children have tested on an average two years ahead of their own age levels. But their main qualification has always been their degree of maturity, compared to that of children elsewhere, even to those much older than themselves.

Recently, during the graduation award ceremonies at a local public high school, one award was withheld to the end. This was for the Most Inspiring Athlete.

Before giving this award, the coach made an unusual speech, of which the following is a paraphrase: "When Michael first entered this school as a freshman, I have to admit I didn't really like him. Nor did I want to work with him.

"Then he went away for a year to study in a private school. When he came back for his junior and senior years, the change in him was tremendous—so much so that, of all our athletes, he quickly stood out as the most inspiring. Four years ago, it wouldn't have entered my mind that, someday, I'd be giving Michael this Most Inspiring Athlete award. Now I feel honored to bestow it on him."

Michael's grades, also, had shown a dramatic improvement after his return.

The private school he attended during his sophomore year was Ananda School. (He remained at Ananda only one year, because he felt a need to "make good" in the school where, initially, he had done badly.)

Over a thousand adults throughout the United States and in Canada have taken courses in what was originally called our "How-to-Live" system of education. The teacher for this course has been Michael Deranja, who developed Ananda's system of education from its beginnings.

In Deranja's experience with the Ananda children, his salient characteristics from the start were the humility to learn from them also, and the compassion to help them according to their individual needs. Without this unusual blend of humility, compassion, and, of course, competence, it is doubtful whether the "Education for Life" system here presented could ever have come into being.

An example of compassion in our schools may be seen in the case of Sandy, who studied at Ananda from the fourth through the eighth grades. When she arrived, her dislike for arithmetic was so intense that any effort to interest her in it would set her sobbing.

Instead of forcing her, Deranja tried to win her gently, by degrees. By the time she left Ananda School, arithmetic—of all subjects!—had become her favorite. It remained so through high school. At the time of high school graduation, when Deranja last saw her, she told him that her dream was to become an accountant.

Compassion has helped to evolve a system that is not dogmatic, and not theoretical, but completely practical.

The remaining question, in considering the living expression of this "Education for Life" system at Ananda, is whether such a system could be made to work in schools everywhere. And the answer needs to be as down-to-earth in its practicality as the system itself. For though most people, perhaps, would like to see at least some of these principles included in the normal school curriculum, it won't do to blind ourselves to the realities.

An elephant is heavier to move than a mouse. Exxon, the largest company in the world, had to spend fifty million dollars merely to change its American name from Esso to Exxon. "The establishment," whether in business, politics, or education, is called that precisely because it *is* so established—entrenched, in fact, in a habit structure perhaps too massive for even revolution to affect it drastically. Minor changes, even, require vast outputs of energy.

I think we must resign ourselves to seeing these "Education for Life" principles widely accepted only gradually, and perhaps not even in our lifetime. Delay, however, should not be cause for discouragement. For such, simply, are life's realities.

I am reminded here of once when Buckminster Fuller, then in his eighties and destined soon to die, was asked by a radio interviewer: "Don't you sometimes get discouraged, talking and writing so much to promote your ideas, but finding so few people willing to accept them?"

"Not at all," Fuller replied with complete equanimity. "New ideas always require at least a generation to become accepted. I know I won't live to see these ideas fulfilled. But I'm confident that future generations will accept them."

Probably, the proposals in this book will gain acceptance, at first, only in private schools, and in relatively small ones at that. Perhaps, indeed, it will be possible to begin only with branches of the Ananda schools. Thus alone may this system be assured a clear and unimpeded beginning. From this beginning, the system may then reach out gradually, perhaps only after decades entering the public school system with any significant force.

The great German physicist, Max Planck, commented wryly that a new scientific concept gains acceptance not so much because of its logical persuasiveness as because the old generation of scientists dies out, and a new generation grows up that is familiar with the concept.

The important thing to realize is that problems with the

initial acceptance of these new concepts in education will very likely not lie in any lack of readiness in the American psyche. Americans generally are desperately aware of the need for a change in the educational system. The problems will lie, rather, in the fact that the mechanics of the system are simply too cumbersome to permit easy alteration.

22

Making It Happen

AN ANANDA CHILD, five years old, once accompanied her mother to a laundromat in nearby Nevada City. There the two of them saw another woman angrily scold her little boy for something quite trivial that he'd done. The Ananda child asked her mother, amazed, "Why is that mommy behaving so badly?"

I posed a question in the last chapter that might be restated thus: Can the "Education for Life" system, developed in a little community on almost the western edge of the North American continent, prove useful to schools in the crowded mainstream of modern life?

And how can the children raised there ever expect to relate realistically, once they grow up, to the Twentieth Century world?

In this book we have defined maturity as the ability to relate to others' realities, and not only to one's own. Is it not necessary, in the light of this definition, to test children's ability to relate to those realities—indeed to familiarize children with them?

The astonishment of that Ananda child, on beholding a grown woman lose her temper, argues an unfamiliarity with a reality to which most Americans have become inured. Is it good, one wonders, for a child to be removed so completely from everyday, if unfortunate, realities?

In short, how does one who has been raised in an atmosphere of love and harmony handle himself, when confronted suddenly with anger and disharmony? Will he not find himself at a serious disadvantage, compared with people for whom selfishness and negativity have always been a simple fact of life?

I am reminded here of someone setting out to read every book ever written, in an effort to master all human knowledge. The task would, of course, be impossible. And even if it weren't, our brains were never made to assimilate such an ocean of information.

The worldly sophisticate, priding himself on the number of facts that he can recall instantly to mind, seldom does more than skate over the frozen surface of reality.

Maturity, defined as the ability to relate to others' realities, doesn't necessarily imply a need to go hunting for an endless number of such realities to which it can relate. The more mature an individual, in fact, the more poised he will be in himself—not selfishly, but like a wheel that is perfectly balanced at its center. The less he will be inclined, therefore, to go searching for fulfillment outside himself.

Maturity means, among other things, a state of inner equilibrium, in which nothing can shake one's poise. Only in such a state of inner balance can one relate effectively to many realities, however foreign they may be to one's expectations.

All of us in this world have to deal with negative emotions in ourselves. It isn't as though anger, fear, belligerence and other human weaknesses were foreign to us, like the corona on the sun. A calm school and home atmosphere, and an education focused on raising a child to emotional maturity, make it easier for him to deal with the negativity in himself. It isn't as if it caused it to cease to exist. On the contrary, it enables him to meet and overcome it.

Once negativity in oneself has been dealt with, rather than merely indulged in, it becomes easier to deal with it objectively in one's encounters with others. The best way to deal with anger, for example, is not to shout back or lose one's own temper, but to meet it with unshakable calmness. The person who is poised in himself can never be conquered. Others will defer to him. And in his presence they will shelve their fury.

We have referred in this book to an expanding awareness as one of the goals of maturity. One might compare this expansion to broadening one's base. The broader the base of a pedestal, the harder it is to knock it over. The more expanded a person's awareness, similarly, the more difficult it is for anyone or anything to upset him.

And who is capable of handling himself most effectively under any circumstance: the person who is easily upset by everything? or the one who remains calm, even in the face of a storm?

As Rudyard Kipling wrote:
"If you can keep your head when all men round you
Are losing theirs and blaming it on you,...
Then you're a man, my son."

The "Education for Life" system taught at Ananda School prepares children to meet challenging situations in another way also. For what one expects from others is very often what he ends up receiving from them. If he doubts their good faith, even the best of them may be at least tempted to justify his negative expectations. But if, on the other hand, he believes in them, even the worst may do their best to justify his belief.

Kindness, good will, a spirit of cooperation, and similar positive traits, if manifested with energy, are magnetic, and will usually attract from others responses in kind. Even where they fail to do so, moreover, the devastation to oneself is invariably minimized.

The "Education for Life" system proves its validity under the most adverse circumstances. It is provenly practical. It is not a system for the few only—for the isolated, or the "spiritual"; it is for everybody. Whether one lives in the mountains or in city slums, its principles are practicable everywhere.

The question remains: How to adopt this new system?

As we pointed out in the last chapter, it would be simplest, at first, to incorporate an "Education for Life" system into small, private schools. For it is best for those launching a new concept in education to have to deal with a minimum of bureaucratic red tape.

It might even be preferable to start out afresh, with new Ananda schools. Such branches would, one imagines, provide the shortest distance between two points: a straight line from idealistic intention to practical fulfillment.

Many of the ideas in this book, however, though perhaps difficult to incorporate in their entirety into an already-existing situation, might be introduced slowly—perhaps one, or a few, at a time. Much might be accomplished, in fact, in quite a number of communities—especially smaller

175

ones—if the people living in them were sufficiently desperate to bring about a change.

A visit to Ananda School would be one obvious way to begin the process. First hand observation is always more instructive than printed theory.

There is also another possibility. A by-product of Ananda School's administration is a team of advisors on the "Education for Life" system. One function of these advisors, known collectively as "Education for Life Associates," is to travel to other communities and give classes and seminars in the principles outlined in this book, as well as to suggest ways in which these principles might be incorporated—wholly, or in part—in other school systems.

If even a few communities in America succeed in adopting these principles, it is our deep belief that a serious start will have been made toward solving many of the deepest problems facing us in American society today.

For further information please write to:

EDUCATION FOR LIFE FOUNDATION
Ananda Village
14618 Tyler Foote Road
Nevada City, CA 95959

Telephone: (916) 292-3775

* * *

I've mentioned in these pages that I have, on occasion, composed music while sitting in the dentist's chair. Not to leave readers with the impression that my habitual source of inspiration is the drill, I should like to add that I've found musical inspiration in more conventional settings as well. Specifically, readers might be interested in a cassette tape of children's songs that I've written and recorded. They express some of the philosophy contained in these pages. The recording is called *Songs of Gladness.* You could order it ($10 postage paid) from:

CRYSTAL HERMITAGE
Ananda Village
14618 Tyler Foote Road
Nevada City, CA 95959

Telephone: (916) 292-3140, or 292-3225